SCIENCE Arts

SCIENCE Arts

Discovering Science
Through Art
Experiences

MARYANN KOHL
JEAN POTTER

Illustrations
K. WHELAN DERY

BRIGHT IDEAS
FOR LEARNING

Bright Ring
Publishing

CREDITS

Illustrations:	K. Whelan Dery
Science Editor:	Suzanne Marchisio
Typography:	textype

ISBN 0-935607-04-8

Library of Congress Catalog Card Number: 93-90056

Copyright © 1993 MaryAnn F. Kohl

Manufactured in the United States of America   1st printing 1993

10   9   8   7   6   5   4   3   2   1

ATTENTION: SCHOOLS AND BUSINESSES

Bright Ring Publishing books are available for quantity discounts with bulk purchase for educational, business, or sales promotional use. For information, please contact:

BRIGHT RING PUBLISHING
P.O. Box 5768
Bellingham, WA 98227 USA
206-734-1601 • FAX 206-676-1271

Publisher's Cataloging in Publication
(Prepared by Quality Books Inc.)

Kohl, MaryAnn F.
    Science arts : discovering science through art / MaryAnn F. Kohl, Jean Potter ; illustrations, K. Whelan Dery.
    p. cm. -- (Bright ideas for learning ; 4)
    Includes bibliographical references and indexes.
    ISBN 0-935607-04-8

    1. Science--Study and teaching (Elementary). 2. Activity programs in education. I. Potter, Jean, 1947- II. Dery, K. Whelan, ill. III. Title. IV. Series: Kohl, MaryAnn F. Bright ideas for learning centers ; 4.

                                                    QBI93-20423

DEDICATION

To my husband, Michael. – *MAK*

To Mary, with devotion and gratitude. – *JP*

ACKNOWLEDGEMENTS

Special thanks to Suzanne Marchisio, science teacher at Whatcom Middle School, Bellingham, WA, for her scientific interpretations of the art experiences as Science Editor for *ScienceArts*. Thanks also to Suzanne's 8th grade 1992-1993 science students for helping write the scientific explanations found on each page of this book.

The following people deserve to be recognized:
    Trish Lemon and Dorothy Tjoelker-Worthen from *textype* for their skill in typesetting, design, and especially their humor during deadlines.
    Charlotte Hart, Hart Design, for her assistance with cover design and photography.
    Matt Brown, Photographer, for his expertise in photography for the front and back covers.
    Donna Shankleton and Ray Sevin, BookCrafters, for all their help with quality printing concerns and the inevitable special favors.
    Students of preschools and elementary schools in the Bellingham area for testing art experiments.

Special thanks from MaryAnn to:
    Amy Cheney, student, Silver Beach Elementary School, for her work as model for the back cover and for her development and submission of the art project, Crayon Creatures. Amy's chauffeur, Joyce Cheney, also deserves thanks for spending hours driving to and from, waiting during, and assisting with the photography session.
    All my closest friends for motivating and inspiring me to keep creating, especially Peggy Campbell, Bonnie Stafford, and Jo Martens.
    My husband, Michael, and my daughters, Hannah and Megan, for their expert creative opinions and advice, and especially their love and support.

Special thanks from Jean to:
    Thomas, my husband, for his constant encouragement and love.
    Archie, for the time I spent in writing, rather than walking him.
    Banff Springs Resort, where most of my ideas were written.
    Macintosh Powerbook, for making my life easier and more mobile.

USING THE ICONS

In the upper page corner of each project, symbolic graphics or *icons* are found which make the projects in **ScienceArts** more usable and accessible. These symbols quickly help identify which projects are appropriate for specific needs and uses of each child and each parent, teacher or care provider.

The icons are suggestions. Experiment with individual techniques or change projects to suit the needs and abilities of children, parents, or teachers. Discovery and experimentation are the key to learning and exploring science through art.

 Age Suggestion
– Indicates a general age range where a child can create and explore without adult assistance. Children younger or older than the age suggested may also enjoy the project. This icon is an indicator of the difficulty of a project; younger ages suggest easy projects and older ages suggest more difficult projects.

draw/color	paint/inks	mixture	sculpture	construction

Art Technique
– Indicates the type of art medium or technique featured in the science/art experience.

easy	moderate	involved

Planning/Preparation
– Indicates the degree of planning or preparation involved in collecting materials and setting up this activity for the adult in charge, from easy to involved.

m	*j*

Author's Favorite
– Indicates the authors' favorite projects shown with an "m" for MaryAnn Kohl's favorites and a "j" for Jean Potter's favorites.

Heat
– Indicates that the activity needs an oven, stove, or other heating element.

 Magnifying Glass
– Indicates the scientific explanation of what happened in the art experiment. It also includes one science concept for each art experiment.

Summer   Fall   Winter   Spring

Seasons
– Indicates the project is particularly well suited to one of the four seasons. Projects that work for all seasons do not carry a seasonal icon.

Science Concept
– Just below the icons, a single science concept is provided to help the reader or the scientific artist understand the concept word inherent in the art experiment. For instance, when working with oil and water, the word *insoluble* is found at the top of the page because it best describes the scientific component of the art idea. Most of these science concepts are also found in the Concept Index.

 Outdoors
– Indicates the use of outdoors in either preparation or in use. Some projects specifically require warm day, freezing night, area with sandbox, area with tree, etc.

 Help
– Indicates a child may need assistance from another child or an adult.

 Caution
– Indicates the use of sharp, hot, or electrical materials where extra care and supervision should be observed with children. Adults should generally do the steps where the caution icon is positioned.

CHART OF CONTENTS

◆ = Easy
◆◆ = Moderate
◆◆◆ = Involved

S = Summer
F = Fall
W = Winter
SP = Spring

M = MaryAnn Kohl favorite
J = Jean Potter favorite

See pages 6 & 7 for icon definitions

Title	Page	Age (3&up)	pen	brush	bowl	bottle	scissors	Difficulty	Season	Favorite	stove	tree	hand
Chapter 1: Water & Air	13												
Wet Paint Design	14	4		●				◆					
Wet and Dry Painting	15	4		●				◆◆		J			
Invisible Designs	16	3		●				◆		J			
Water Painting	17	3		●				◆	S			●	
Oil & Water Painting	18	4		●				◆◆					
Oil Painting	19	5		●				◆◆					
Frost Plate	20	3	●					◆	W				
Frozen Paper	21	7		●				◆◆	W			●	
Cube Painting	22	3		●				◆◆					
Colored Ice Cubes	23	4		●				◆		J		●	
Rain Dancer	24	4		●				◆	SP			●	
Chalk Float Design	25	8	●					◆◆					
Ice Structures	26	5				●		◆◆	W			●	
Ice & Salt Sculpture	27	8				●		◆◆		M			
Color Bottles	28	4				●		◆					
Bottle Fountain	29	6				●		◆◆	S			●	
Bottle Optics	30	3				●		◆		J			
Water Tube	31	8				●		◆◆◆	S			●	●
Flowing Patterns	32	7			●			◆					
Paper Molds	33	7			●			◆◆					●
Floating Sculpture	34	7				●		◆◆					
Clay Floats	35	7				●		◆◆					
Color Waves	36	3			●			◆		M			
Crystal Sparkle Dough	37	3			●			◆◆					
Straw Painting	38	5		●				◆					
Streamer Rings	39	6				●		◆◆	F			●	
Wind Chatcher	40	6					●	◆◆	F			●	
Windy Wrap	41	6				●		◆◆	F			●	
Wind Chime	42	7				●		◆◆	SP			●	
Chapter 2: Light & Sight	43												
Spinning Designs	44	7	●					◆					
Hidden Coloring	45	6	●					◆					
Secret Pictures	46	7		●				◆◆					●
Stretch Picture	47	7					●	◆				●	
Dot Matrix Picture	48	8		●				◆◆		M			
Face Illusions	49	8	●					◆◆					
Tissue Color Mix	50	5					●	◆					

Title	Page	3 & up	✏️	🖌️	🥣	🕯️	✂️	◐	☀️	m	🍳	🌳	✋
Immiscibles	96	7			●			◆◆					
Chromatography	97	9		●				◆◆◆					●
Erupting Colors	98	8			●			◆◆		M			●
The Volcano	99	9			●			◆◆	S			●	
Crystal Design	100	9			●			◆◆◆					●
Crystal Paint	101	4		●				◆	W	M			
Crystal Bubbles	102	4			●			◆◆	W	M			
Crystal Needles	103	7			●			◆◆					
Crystal Ink	104	8	●					◆				●	●
Plastic Milk	105	9			●			◆◆◆				●	●
Marshmallow Tower	106	6					●	◆		M			
Building Beans	107	5					●	◆					
Spaghetti Painting	108	3		●				◆		J		●	
Sandpaper Designs	109	3	●					◆					
Invisible Paint	110	3		●				◆					
Magic Cabbage	111	5	●					◆◆				●	●
Sculptured Pretzels	112	4			●			◆◆				●	●
Chapter 5: Nature & Earth	113												
Bark Rubbings	114	4		●				◆◆	SP			●	
Shoe Polish Leaves	115	5		●				◆	F			●	
Nature Spray	116	6		●				◆◆	SP			●	
Plant Imprints	117	3					●	◆	SP	J		●	
Symmetry Prints	118	5		●				◆		J			●
Sticky Pictures	119	3					●	◆	S			●	
Stencil Leaves	120	6		●				◆◆	F			●	
Tree Arts	121	8		●				◆	S			●	
Indoor Bird Tracks	122	5	●					◆					
Grass Patterns	123	5					●	◆	SP	J		●	
Sand Drawings	124	6	●					◆◆		M			
Sand Garden	125	3				●		◆◆	S			●	
Dried Seaweed Print	126	8					●	◆◆◆	S				●
Dried Arrangement	127	8				●		◆◆	F				●
Nature Windows	128	4					●	◆◆	F			●	●
Garden Sculpture	129	3				●		◆◆	SP	M			
Food Paints	130	4		●				◆◆	S				
Home Paints	131	6		●				◆◆◆	SP				
Sand Clay	132	7			●			◆				●	●

INTRODUCTION

ScienceArts provides children with an exciting opportunity to learn basic science concepts through art experiences. Children ages three through ten can explore the hands-on activities in each *ScienceArts* experiment. While exploring with art materials, children also experience basic science concepts.

Children explore, manipulate, and discover art and science as an intertwined process rather than a final product. Thus the product becomes an outcome of experimenting and experiencing, rather than the sole reason for the activity. The pure joy of discovery and taking an active part in learning is the main objective of *ScienceArts*.

ScienceArts appeals to the combination of the curiosity of science and the beauty of art. Each art activity has a science concept inherent in its process. Science experiments many times are filled with interesting and amazing reactions, effects, and results. Thus, children are not only captured with the beauty and fun of the creation, but may also be fascinated and surprised with the scientific components.

Each page of *ScienceArts* contains one recipe style experiment which includes simple instructions, clear illustrations, and suggestions for variations or extensions to enhance learning. Each is designed to be used by an individual child or by small groups of children usually independently and sometimes with minimal adult help. Materials needed for each experiment are commonly found in most homes or classrooms making *ScienceArts* ideal for home or school use.

ScienceArts is simple to use. Each page contains a variety of information to assist the reader in selecting an appropriate experiment. Icons on each page include age guidelines, materials needed, seasonal suggestions, help needed, and authors' favorites. Variations are included to extend the activity for new and enriching experiments. Explanations of science concepts are also included to assist both children and adults in understanding the connection between art and science.

Also included is a detailed Chart of Contents to assist in selecting appropriate projects for specific needs and a Concept Index with explanations of new words and scientific vocabulary. Two additional indexes provide a helpful way to find experiments by materials on hand or by alphabetical listings. A detailed list of resource books is included for those who wish to augment experiences in *ScienceArts*.

Every child loves to explore, experiment, and discover. *ScienceArts* builds on the natural curiosity of each child while combining the beauty of art and the fascination of science. Even those with a limited understanding of science will feel comfortable with the activities in *ScienceArts* as they are delivered through the familiar forum of process art.

Discover the beauty, the magic, the amazement, and the satisfaction of creating and experiencing science through art and art through science.

"The fairest thing we can experience is the mysterious. It is the fundamental emotion which stands at the cradle of true art and true science."
– Albert Einstein

WATER AND AIR
chapter 1

WET PAINT DESIGN

DIFFUSION

MATERIALS:
water
shallow pan
cookie sheet with sides
tempera paint, thinned with water
eyedroppers
construction paper
newspaper

ART EXPERIMENT:
1. Wet the paper thoroughly by dipping it into the pan of water.
2. Place the wet paper immediately on the cookie sheet.
3. Drop different colors of thinned tempera paint on the wet paper using the eyedroppers.
4. Remove the painting from the cookie sheet to newspaper to dry.

VARIATIONS:
- Instead of eyedroppers, dip other objects in the paint:
  – cotton swab
  – paint brush
  – drinking straw
  – feather
  – twig
- Draw with colored chalk on wet paper.
- Use water-based colored marking pens on wet paper.
- Use watercolor paints instead of tempera paints on wet paper.

When a drop of paint is added to a wet piece of paper, the paint molecules slowly DIFFUSE or spread out in the water on the paper. DIFFUSION occurs when the paint molecules are crowded into one spot on the wet paper as a drop, but gradually spread out in the water.

WET AND DRY PAINTING

MATERIALS:

water
shallow pan
cookie pan with sides
tempera paints, powdered
several salt shakers
construction paper
newspaper

ART EXPERIMENT:
1. Put the dry tempera paint into a salt shaker and shake it to see if the paint comes out. Do the same for the other shakers and paint colors.
2. Fill the shallow cookie pan half full with water.
3. Wet the paper thoroughly by dipping it into the pan of water and place it immediately in the cookie pan.
4. Shake different colors of the dry tempera on the wet paper.
5. Remove the paper from the pan and let it dry on newspaper.

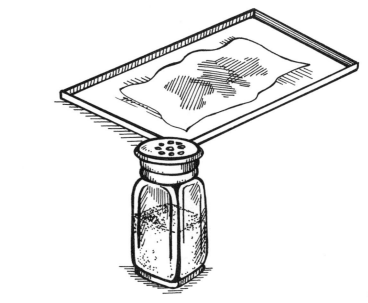

VARIATIONS:
- Color a picture on construction paper first, and then apply water and dry paint from a shaker.
- Shake salt on the Wet and Dry Painting to see the crystals react with water.
- Sprinkle dry paint on dry paper. Then go outside into the rain and let the drops of rain spatter the paint.

> *As powdered tempera paint is shaken onto the wet paper, the paint particles are* ABSORBED *by the water and then begin to* DISSOLVE. *The liquid paint will then* DIFFUSE *and spread throughout the water forming designs and patterns.*

INVISIBLE DESIGNS

INSOLUBLE

MATERIALS:
cooking oil in cup
butcher paper
brushes
water in cup
window or light source

ART EXPERIMENT:
1. Paint with cooking oil on butcher paper.
2. Hold the design up to the light to make the art visible.
3. With a paint brush full of water, paint over the oil design. Paint on the untouched paper too.
4. Look at the way oil and water act together.

VARIATIONS:
* Using a damp sponge, try to wipe the oil design away.
* Paint with watercolors on the oil and water designs.
* Draw with permanent felt pens on the oil and water designs.

Oil and water are INSOLUBLE *which means they will not mix. When oil is brushed on the butcher paper, it is* ABSORBED *by the paper or soaks into the paper and will not mix with the water. But wherever there is no oil on the paper, the water easily absorbs into the paper.*

WATER PAINTING

MATERIALS:
bucket
house painting brushes
water
outdoor area with sidewalks, rocks, or buildings

ART EXPERIMENT:
1. Fill the bucket with water.
2. Dip the brush into the water.
3. Work outdoors, painting sidewalks, sides of buildings, rocks, concrete or asphalt play areas, swing sets, and more.
4. Paint designs or simply paint to cover objects with a bright, shiny coat of water.
5. When the water evaporates or dries, paint the objects again.

VARIATIONS:
- Mark the water level in the bucket with a pen. Leave the bucket outside all day. Check the new water level after the water has evaporated some.
- Wash doll clothes and hang to dry, observing evaporation.

When water, a liquid, is brushed onto a surface like a rock, it will usually change into water vapor, a gas, and enter the air. This process of change is called EVAPORATION. When the air gets full of water vapor or when the water vapor cools down, it changes to a liquid again in the form of rain.

OIL & WATER PAINTING

DENSITY / INSOLUBLE

MATERIALS:
paper
cooking oil
2 colors of tempera paint
2 (500 ml) cups
2 eyedroppers
water
spoons
baking pan with sides

ART EXPERIMENT:
1. Mix one color of paint with water in a cup until thin and watery.
2. Mix the second color of paint with oil in the other cup.
3. Place a sheet of paper in the baking pan.
4. Next use one eyedropper to drip spots of the watery paint onto the paper.
5. Then use the second eyedropper to drip spots of oily paint on top of the watery paint spots.
6. Tip the pan back and forth to move the paints. The oil paint will float on the water paint to create unusual effects.

VARIATIONS:
- Use more colors of paints.
- Use a variety of paper textures.
- Use a larger tray or pan, larger paper, and a turkey baster instead of en eyedropper.

Oil and water will not mix and are said to be INSOLUBLE. When the oily paint is dripped on the watery paint, the two liquids stay separate and arrange themselves in layers according to their DENSITY. The watery paint is most dense and forms the bottom layer; the oily paint is least dense and floats on the water as the top layer.

OIL PAINTING

MATERIALS:
vegetable oil
tempera paint, powdered
paper
shallow cake pan
water
spoons
cups
newspaper

ART EXPERIMENT:
1. Mix the tempera paint and oil in a cup until creamy.
2. Fill the cake pan about 1/2 full with water.
3. Spoon a few drops of the oil paint mixture on top of the water.
4. Use a spoon to gently swirl the paint.
5. Next, lay a piece of paper on top of the water and oil paint.
   Let the paper float for a minute or so.
6. Carefully lift the paper by one corner.
7. Immediately place the painting on newspaper to dry.

VARIATIONS:
- Use Oil Painting designs as note cards, book covers, or wrapping paper.
- Create Oil Painting on waxed paper, paper plates, or plastic wrap.
- Add glitter on top of the wet oil paint.
- Mix salt and dry tempera to make a glittery paint.

> *Oil and water won't mix because they are* INSOLUBLE. *The oily paint floats on top of the water in the pan because the water is denser than oil. Oil will not* DISSOLVE *in water; oil stays oil and water stays water.*

FROST PLATE

CRYSTALS / FREEZING

MATERIALS:
petroleum jelly
clear glass pie plate
freezer

ART EXPERIMENT:
1. Smear petroleum jelly on the glass pie plate.
2. Draw a design in the jelly on the plate with fingers.
3. Clean hands.
4. Put the plate in the freezer for 2 hours.
5. Remove the plate and look at the frost designs.

Water is a unique substance because it can be ice (a solid), water (a liquid), or water vapor (a gas), all within a close range of temperatures. When the petroleum jelly is placed in the freezer, water vapor in the freezer FREEZES and crystallizes on the jelly where it is easily seen in the drawing. The water vapor molecules slow down when cooled to 32 ˚F (0 ˚C) or below, and arrange themselves in a regular pattern on the petroleum jelly as they form ice CRYSTALS.

FROZEN PAPER

MATERIALS:
freezer (or freezing day outdoors)
heavy paper
water
shallow pan
cookie sheet
watercolor paints and brush

ART EXPERIMENT:
1. Dip the paper in a shallow pan of water until it's thoroughly wet.
2. Place the wet paper on a cookie sheet.
3. Place the cookie sheet and paper in the freezer or outside to freeze.
4. When frozen, remove the paper from the freezer and paint on the paper before it thaws.

VARIATIONS:
- Freeze a different variety of papers for painting – paper towel, coffee filter, construction paper, typing paper.
- Draw with chalk on frozen paper.
- Paint with tempera paints on frozen paper.

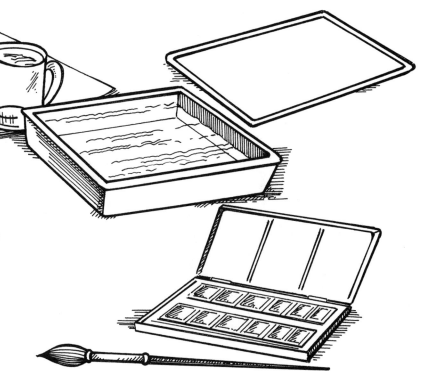

 When watercolor paint comes in contact with the FROZEN *paper, it cools and nearly freezes too. This cooling slows down the movement of the paint molecules and the paint begins to freeze and behave more like a solid. If the paper begins to thaw or melt, the molecules of paint and water move faster and mix more easily, much like the usual behavior of paint and water.*

CUBE PAINTING

FREEZING / MELTING

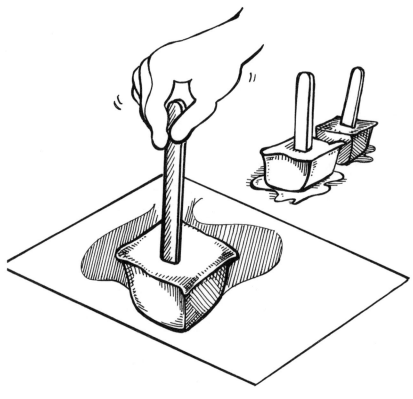

MATERIALS:
2 measuring cups
plastic ice cube trays
water
2 colors of tempera paint
craft sticks
white drawing paper
freezer
paper

ART EXPERIMENT:
1. Mix one color tempera paint with water in a measuring cup and the second color tempera paint with water in the other measuring cup. Mix until thin and lightly colored.
2. Pour the paint into plastic ice cube trays.
3. Put a craft stick in each cube section.
4. Freeze the tempera water mixture.
5. When frozen, remove the cubes from the trays.
6. Hold the stick of the tempera paint ice cubes and paint a picture on the white drawing paper.

VARIATIONS:
• Make the frozen paint cubes in a muffin tin.
• Make additional colors of ice cubes.

When the water and paint mixture is cooled to 32 ˚F (0 ˚C) or lower, it FREEZES or changes from a liquid to a solid. Then when the paint ice cube is removed from the freezer, it begins to MELT because the temperature is higher than 32 ˚F (0 ˚C). The ice melts into liquid paint as it is spread over the paper with the craft stick handle.

COLORED ICE CUBES

MATERIALS:

variety of food colorings
water
plastic ice cube tray
freezer
paper
cups
spoon
warm day outdoors

ART EXPERIMENT:

1. Mix each food coloring with water in a cup.
2. Pour the different colors of water in the individual compartments of plastic ice cube trays filling them 1/4 full.
3. Place in the freezer until frozen solid.
4. Remove the colored cubes from the trays.
5. Take the paper and the trays outside.
6. Arrange the cubes on the paper and let them melt and mix colors.
7. Then dry the colored cube picture completely.

VARIATIONS:

- Put craft sticks in the ice cube compartments before freezing. When frozen, paint with the colored ice cubes on sticks.
- Use 1 ice cube and move the paper around so the cube does the painting.

When the colored water is placed in the freezer at 32 °F (0 °C) or lower, it begins to change from a liquid to a solid. In a short period of time, the molecules of water slow down until the water FREEZES in its solid state – ice. As soon as the ice is carried outside where the temperature is higher than 32 °F (0 °C), it begins to MELT or change to its liquid state – water. Because the water is colored and not clear, patterns and swirls of colors mix and run together as the ice melts and spreads out on the paper.

RAIN DANCER

DIFFUSION

MATERIALS:
rainy day outdoors
white construction paper
tempera paints
paintbrushes

ART EXPERIMENT:
1. Paint with tempera paints on the white paper.
2. Take the painting outside and place it on the ground face up so the rain drops land on it.
3. When ready, take the rainy painting inside to dry.

VARIATIONS:
• Carry blank, dry paper into the rain. Return indoors and paint on wet paper.
• Put small sprinkles of dry tempera on the paper and let the rain sprinkle on the dry paint.
• Paint on paper. Then spray water from a spray bottle on the painting.

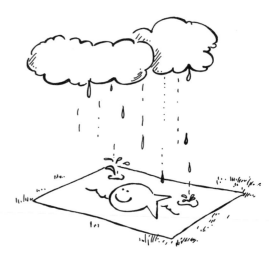

When the painting is carried out into the rain, the rain drops hit the paint with an even sprinkling of water. Where each drop of rain hits, the paint is thinned or spread out and DIFFUSED. *In this experiment* DIFFUSION *is the gradual mixing of paint molecules and water molecules. The diffusion of water and paint on the paper forms patterns and designs in the dry paint areas.*

CHALK FLOAT DESIGN

MATERIALS:
construction paper
colored chalk
large cake pan half-filled with water
kitchen grater
water

ART EXPERIMENT:
1. Grate the colored chalk into very fine pieces on a piece of paper.
2. Sprinkle the colored chalk gratings on the water in the pan.
3. Carefully float the construction paper on the water.
4. Lift the paper out of the water and look at the chalk designs.
5. Place the chalk float picture in a place where it will dry overnight.

VARIATIONS:
- Dip corners of a piece of paper through the floating chalk.
- Completely dip small pieces of paper into a bucket of water with chalk floating on the surface. Cover both sides of the paper.

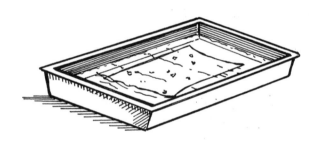

A stick of chalk would normally sink in a pan of water, but floats when it is shaved into hundreds of tiny bits. Water forms a "skin" on its surface which holds up objects that usually sink. This "skin" caused by water molecules that line up and are strongly attracted to each other is called SURFACE TENSION. *The chalk bits are so small and light that the surface tension of the water holds them up on the surface.*

ICE STRUCTURES

FREEZING

MATERIALS:
food coloring
variety of molds –
    yogurt cups, muffin pan, ice cube tray, candy molds
snow
large pail
freezing day outdoors

ART EXPERIMENT:
1. Mix water with food coloring in a large pail.
2. Pour the colored water into the molds.
3. Leave the molds outside to freeze.
4. When frozen, bring the molds inside.
5. Let the frozen molds thaw a little at room temperature to remove the ice shapes more easily.
6. Then take the ice shapes outside and build a sculpture using the ice shapes and use small amounts of snow like glue or cement. Freeze.

> *If the temperature is 32 °F (0 °C) or below, water will FREEZE in its solid form – ice. At these low temperatures, the water molecules move very slowly and gradually come together in a regular pattern called ICE.*

ICE & SALT SCULPTURE

MATERIALS:
large chunk of ice
    (freeze water in a large mixing bowl the day before)
3/4 cup (190 ml) salt
food coloring
1/4 cup (60 ml) warm water
spray bottles, set on "stream"
baking pan
scissors

ART EXPERIMENT:
1. Place the ice chunk in a baking pan.
2. In a plastic spray bottle, mix 1/4 cup warm water with food coloring and 3/4 cup salt. Make at least two different spray bottles and colors. Set aside.
3. Pour a cup of water over the ice chunk to make it slick.
4. Next, squirt the warm, salty colored water on the ice chunk. Be sure the bottle is set on "stream," not "spray."
5. Squirt small amounts of liquid on different areas of the ice. (If too much gets on one area, rinse with clear water.) Try to form caverns, holes, cracks, and designs.
6. The ice sculpture is complete when the ice chunk is filled with designs and colors as desired.

VARIATIONS:
- Make more than two colors of spray bottles for more color contrasts.
- Experiment with different sizes of ice chunks.
- Try this experiment without the salt and see what happens.

> *Every substance has a MELTING POINT, the temperature at which that substance will begin to change from a solid to a liquid. The melting point of ice is 32 °F (0 °C). But when salt is DISSOLVED in water and sprayed on the ice chunk, the melting point of the ice is lowered and the ice melts more quickly.*

COLOR BOTTLES

DIFFUSION

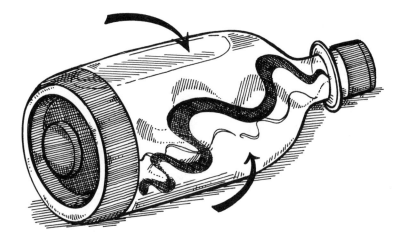

MATERIALS:
plastic bottle with cap (soda or mineral water)
water
food coloring
newspaper or towel for spills
table

ART EXPERIMENT:
1. Fill the plastic bottle with water.
2. Add a few drops of red food coloring to the water in the bottle.
3. Place the cap on the bottle tightly.
4. Roll the bottle back and forth across the table and watch the color diffuse through the water.
5. Uncap the bottle and add a few drops of blue.
6. Repeat the rolling process and observe the new color.
7. Now add a few drops of yellow to the red and blue, rolling as before to see diffusion of color in the water.

VARIATIONS:
• Mix blue and yellow only.
• Mix yellow and red only.
• Save bottles for decoration in a sunny window.
• Use other bottles, jars, and transparent containers.

Food coloring mixes with water in the plastic bottle in a slow process called DIFFUSION. When the red food coloring is first dropped into the water, the molecules are crowded together. Then the food coloring molecules gradually spread throughout the water and the molecules have more space. The more the red color DIFFUSES, the lighter the color of the water will be because the color spreads out more and more. Rolling the bottles and causing the water to move around speeds up the process of diffusion and the molecules move about more quickly.

BOTTLE FOUNTAIN

PRESSURE

MATERIALS:
empty dishwashing soap bottle
thumbtack or nail
water
bucket or sink
outdoor area
towel

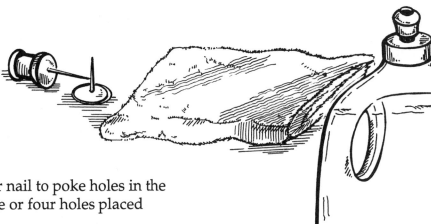

ART EXPERIMENT:
1. Working outdoors, use the thumbtack or nail to poke holes in the dishwashing soap bottle. Start with three or four holes placed high and low.
2. Holding the bottle over a sink or bucket, fill the bottle with water.
3. Watch the water flow in different fountain jets.
4. After observing the water fountain jet design, add more holes until a desired fountain is acheived.
5. Add more water.
6. Watch the new fountain jet shapes.
7. Use the towel for any clean up.

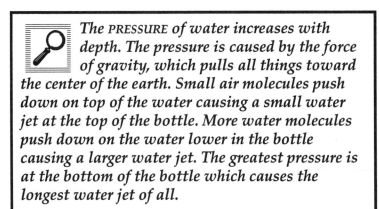

VARIATION:
- Stand a plastic bottle on a sidewalk outside and poke only one hole in the bottle. Then pour water into the spout and watch how far the water jets. Poke a second hole in a different spot and see how the second jet compares to the first. Continue adding holes in different places and comparing.

> *The PRESSURE of water increases with depth. The pressure is caused by the force of gravity, which pulls all things toward the center of the earth. Small air molecules push down on top of the water causing a small water jet at the top of the bottle. More water molecules push down on the water lower in the bottle causing a larger water jet. The greatest pressure is at the bottom of the bottle which causes the longest water jet of all.*

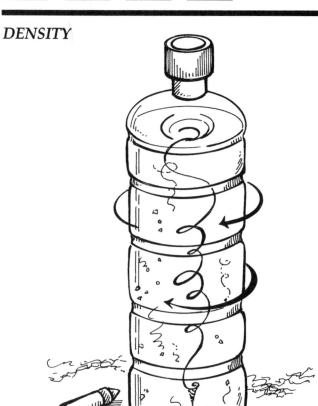

BOTTLE OPTICS

DENSITY

MATERIALS:
large, clear plastic bottle (from mineral water or soda)
water
crayon shavings
glitter
metal or plastic confetti
bits of Easter grass

ART EXPERIMENT:
1. Fill the bottle with water.
2. Add crayon shavings, glitter, or other small floating materials such as bits of Easter grass or plastic confetti.
3. Replace the lid and tighten.
4. Shake the bottle and watch the objects move.
5. Try to make a tornado movement by swirling in one direction.
6. Experiment with designs and patterns in movement by tipping and shaking the bottle different ways.

VARIATIONS:
- Color the water with food coloring.
- Use objects which float and sink and observe how they react to the moving water.

Lightweight, tiny materials like crayon shavings and glitter that have the same DENSITY as water will be carried around with the moving water. These materials do not float on top of the water or sink to the bottom of the water but are suspended in the water and move around freely when the bottle is shaken and swirled.

WATER TUBE

MATERIALS:
two pieces of transparent flexible tubing:
   3 feet (1 m) of 1" tubing
   6 inches (15 cm) of 1/2" tubing
glitter
water
scissors
outdoor play area

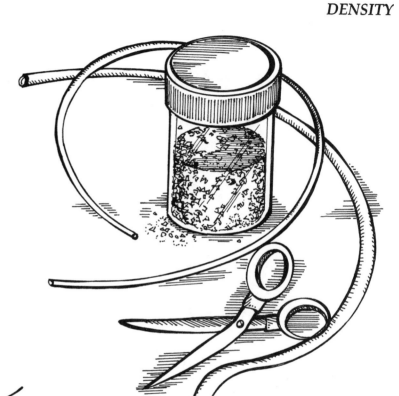

ART EXPERIMENT:
1. Cut the 1" tube into a 3 ft. length.
2. Put some glitter in one end of the tube while holding the other end.
3. Put enough water in the tube to fill it 3/4 full while continuing to hold the other end up.
4. Cut a 6" piece of the 1/2" tube.
5. Put the smaller tubing inside both ends of the larger tubing forming a circle and a sort of plug.
6. Shake and move the water tube to see floating, sinking, swirling glitter.

VARIATIONS:
- Find small objects like buttons, nuts and bolts to fit inside the tube.
- Put soap and water inside the tube and shake.

The small bits of glitter are carried along in the water in the clear plastic tube because glitter has about the same DENSITY *as the water. The glitter is cut into tiny pieces that are thin and flat. The water molecules push the flat surface of a piece of glitter, supporting it like a feather floating in the air.*

FLOWING PATTERNS

SYMMETRY

MATERIALS:
shallow baking pan
water
6 t. (30 ml) cornstarch
food coloring in squeeze bottles
stick or straw

ART EXPERIMENT:
1. Fill the baking pan with water about 1" deep.
2. Add the cornstarch to the water one spoonful at a time and stir until the mixture looks milky.
3. Drop one drop of blue food coloring in the middle of the pan.
4. Next, slowly drag a stick through the color in a straight line. Watch patterns and designs form.
5. Now add one drop of yellow near the center of the pan, and one drop of red two inches away from the blue drop.
6. Watch new patterns and designs form while dragging the stick slowly between these two drops of food coloring.
7. Continue to create flowing patterns by dropping color in different places on the water and moving the stick through the colors.

VARIATIONS:
- Use a variety of other colors.
- Add several drops of cooking oil to the cornstarch water.

Liquids make designs as they flow and patterns as they flow into each other. SYMMETRY *occurs in the water and cornstarch mixture when a straight line is drawn through the color drop and identical patterns form on either side of the line. In other words, the two sides of the design are* SYMMETRICAL *or matching halves.*

PAPER MOLDS

MATERIALS:

measuring cups   strainer
water   spray vegetable oil
torn newspaper   candy molds
torn colored tissue paper   sponge
blender   paper towels

◆ adult help

ART EXPERIMENT:

1. Mix 3-1/2 (875 ml) to 4 cups (1 l) water with 1/4 cup (62.5 ml) torn newspaper pieces in a blender.
2. Add some torn tissue paper for more color. Put on the lid and blend.
3. Strain the watery paper pulp, removing as much water as possible.
4. Spray some oil on the candy molds.
5. Press the paper pulp in the molds evenly.
6. Blot the pulp with a sponge to remove excess water.
7. Place a paper towel on top of the molds.
8. Place the molds in a warm place and dry thoroughly.
9. Remove the dried colorful paper pulp forms from the molds.

VARIATIONS:

- Other items can be added to the blending stage of this project such as glitter, pieces of construction paper, or bits of grass.
- The dried paper molds can be used as beads for a necklace, pendants, or holiday decorations.

EVAPORATION

Paper is made from tiny fibers intertwined and pressed together. Soaking the torn paper in water and then blending it breaks the paper into fibers again. Paper-makers call this wet mass a 'slurry.' The paper will reform into a dry solid when the water EVAPORATES from the slurry and hold the shape of the candy mold. EVAPORATION is the change of water from a liquid to a gas, which then escapes into the air. Warming the paper molds speeds up the process of evaporation by speeding up the movement of water molecules. The faster the water molecules move, the faster they change into gas, leave the paper, and enter the air. The paper molds are then dry.

FLOATING SCULPTURE

BUOYANCY

MATERIALS:
floating objects such as –
> craft sticks, corks, styrofoam bits, foil, sponges, straws, wood shavings, pieces of clay shaped like boats, thread, etc.

scissors
baking pan
water
towel to dry hands

ART EXPERIMENT:
1. Fill the baking pan with water about 3/4 full.
2. Test the flotation of objects. See which ones float and which ones sink.
3. Begin floating objects in the pan. Add more objects until a floating sculpture is complete.

VARIATIONS:
*   Stir the sculpture to watch objects move and change.
*   Glue a variety of objects together with white glue. Dry. Float this entire sculpture in a pan, bowl, or tub depending on it's size and the depth of water needed.
*   Use scraps of wood for a wood sculpture.

> *Objects like corks and bits of wood float in water because the water molecules push up on the objects more than gravity pulls them down. The upthrust of the water is called* BUOYANCY. FLOTATION *occurs when the upthrust of water is in balance with the* DENSITY *of the objects. If an object is dense and pushes down more than the water pushes up, the object will sink.*

34   water and air

CLAY FLOATS

MATERIALS:
modeling clay or plasticine
marbles
paper clips
deep baking pan half-filled with water
toothpicks
paper scraps
glue

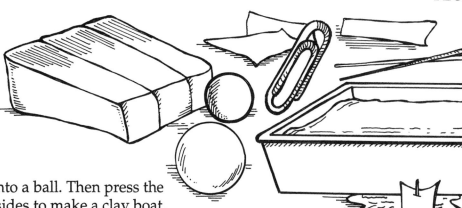

ART EXPERIMENT:
1. Roll a small amount of modeling clay into a ball. Then press the ball into a flat piece. Next, turn up the sides to make a clay boat.
2. Form bits of clay into other floating shapes.
3. Experiment with placing marbles and paper clips in the clay boats to see which ones will float or sink.
4. Make little sails of paper scraps glued to toothpicks to stick in the clay boats. Blow on the paper sails and see if the clay boats move.

VARIATIONS:
- Find other materials that will float such as jar lids, styrofoam trays, and bottle caps.
- Make boats out of reused aluminum foil.

Any substance like a ball of clay or a brick is DENSER than water and will SINK. A ball of clay sinks because it pushes down on the water more than the water pushes up on the clay. To make the dense clay ball FLOAT, it can be shaped into a cup, bowl, or boat which increases the volume of water the clay DISPLACES. If there is a balance between the pushing of the clay and the upthrust of the water, the clay will float. Adding marbles or paper clips to the clay boat adds weight. If the water pushes up more than the weighted boat pushes down, the boat will float.

COLOR WAVES

INSOLUBLE / EMULSION

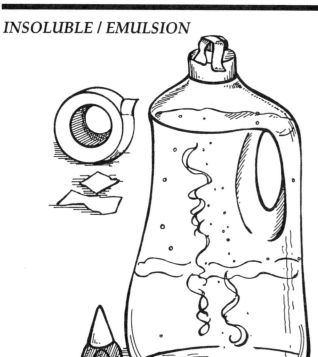

MATERIALS:
clear plastic bottle with cap
water
food coloring
baby oil
masking tape

ART EXPERIMENT:
1. Fill the bottle about 1/3 full with water.
2. Add some food coloring until desired color is reached.
3. Fill the remainder of the bottle with baby oil.
4. Put the cap on the bottle and tape securely.
5. Shake, roll, swirl, and experiment with the bottle of oil and water to make color waves and bubbles.

VARIATIONS:
- Add other items to the Color Waves such as glitter, crayon shavings, or bits of plastic confetti.
- Add liquid dishwashing soap to the bottle of oil and colored water. Shake.

The colored water and oil do not mix even though they are in the same container. They can be shaken and briefly combined, but they will separate again if left to rest. Oil and water are INSOLUBLE because they do not mix. When soap is shaken with the oil and colored water, the result is an EMULSION or a suspension of tiny oil globules in the soapy colored water. The soap has simply broken the oil into smaller balls of oil which are suspended throughout the water but are still separate from the water.

CRYSTAL SPARKLE DOUGH

CRYSTALS

MATERIALS:
3 squeeze bottles
3 cups
3 tempera paint colors
equal parts of flour, salt, and water
paper
bowl
spoon

ART EXPERIMENT:
1. Use a spoon to mix equal parts of flour, salt and water in a bowl.
2. Add some tempera paint to the mixture.
3. Divide the mixture and pour into a squeeze bottle.
4. Repeat this procedure with the next two squeeze bottles using different paint colors.
5. Squeeze the paint mixture onto paper in any design.
6. Let the paint dry thoroughly to see the sparkles.

VARIATIONS:
- Work on wood, shells, or cardboard.
- Spread the mixture with a spatula instead of squeezing.
- Vary the size of the holes in other squeeze bottles.

> *Paint, flour, and salt will DISSOLVE in water and can be made into a colorful dough. The particles of paint, flour, and salt break apart and spread evenly throughout the water. As the dough dries, the water EVAPORATES and the flour, salt, and paint become solid again. Salt acts a bit differently than the paint and flour because after salt is dissolved in water, it forms CRYSTALS as it dries and becomes a solid.*

STRAW PAINTING

PRESSURE

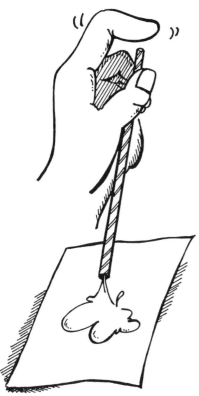

MATERIALS:
drinking straws
tempera paint, thinned and watery
paper
muffin tin

ART EXPERIMENT:
1. Dip the bottom end of a drinking straw in the watery tempera paint while holding a finger over the top end of the straw.
2. Move the straw to the paper and release the paint on the paper by removing the finger from the top end of the straw.
3. Follow the process several times until the Straw Painting is completed.
4. Let the paint dry.

VARIATIONS:
• Enhance the painting by using a paintbrush to move the paints around.
• Add glitter, yarn, ribbon, or fabric scraps to the wet paint.

When the straw is dipped into the paint, some paint is pushed up into the straw by the PRESSURE on the surface of the paint. Air molecules are pushing down on the paint in the straw, too. By putting a finger over the top of the straw, a balance of pressure above and below the paint in the straw is maintained. When the finger is removed from the straw, more air molecules push down on the paint than push up, and the paint comes out.

STREAMER RINGS

MATERIALS:
plastic lid (from coffee, margarine, or shortening tubs)
strips of newspaper, crepe paper, ribbon, or cloth
scissors
tape (optional)
windy day outdoors

WIND

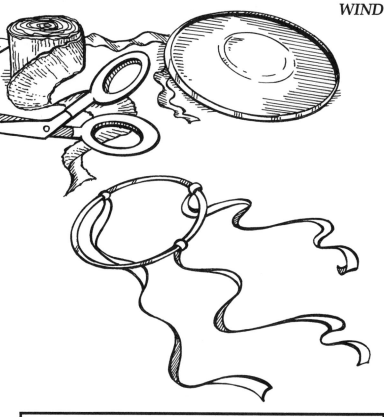

ART EXPERIMENT:
1. Poke the point of a scissors into a plastic lid.
2. Cut a large circle in the lid of the plastic container. Save the rim or edge of the lid. Discard the center circle.
3. Tape or tie strips of newspaper or colorful ribbons and cloth strips to the plastic rim.
4. Hold the decorated rim in the wind and watch the streamers blow.

VARIATIONS:
- Tie many decorated rims to a swing set or tree and watch them blow.
- Tie metal objects to the bottom of the ribbons to make wind chimes when blowing.
- Tie several streamer sculptures to the center of a long rope. With a child holding each end of the rope, run side by side across a field or playground with the rope stretched between.

Lightweight materials like strips of newspaper or pieces of ribbon move easily in the WIND. The direction of the wind is indicated by which way the streamers float. If the streamer floats out to the south, the wind is blowing from the north (called a northerly wind). Wind can be made by running with the streamers. Instead of the wind blowing air past the runner, the runner is moving past the air. The effect on the streamer rings is the same.

WIND CATCHER

WIND

MATERIALS:
oatmeal box
construction paper
glue
crepe paper
scissors
paper punch
string
crayons
windy day outdoors

ART EXPERIMENT:
1. Cut the ends out of the oatmeal box.
2. Decorate the box with construction paper and crayon.
3. Punch several holes in the bottom of the oatmeal box.
4. Cut crepe paper about 3 ft. (2.7 m) long.
5. Lace the crepe paper through these holes and tie.
6. Punch 4 holes in the top of the box.
7. Lace 4 strings through these holes.
8. Tie the strings together and tie these to a longer string.
9. Hang the Wind Catcher outside. Watch the wind go to work.

VARIATIONS:
- Tie strips of fabric, plastic, and other materials to the Wind Catcher.
- Create a Wind Catcher from a potato chip can, margarine tub, or other cylinders and containers.

True windsocks are important indicators of wind direction used at airports and marinas. WIND is made up of moving air molecules, but the wind is invisible. WIND can be felt but not seen. The Wind Catcher makes it possible to tell which direction and how hard the wind is blowing.

WINDY WRAP

MATERIALS:
lightweight fabrics and papers
clothespins
clothesline rope or heavy string
permanent markers
windy day

ART EXPERIMENT:
1. Color the fabrics and papers with permanent markers in a variety of designs.
2. Wrap the clothesline rope through trees, around bushes, over benches and other outdoor environmental objects.
3. Clothespin the light weight materials on the rope so they will blow in the wind.
4. When Windy Wrap has been thoroughly enjoyed, be sure to clean up and recycle the materials.

VARIATIONS:
- Test a variety of materials such as waxed paper, aluminum foil, and plastic bags to see which ones will blow most freely.
- Add recycled items to the Windy Wrap such as plastic 6-pack rings, bottle caps, styrofoam trays, and paper cups.

Although air is invisible, it is made up of tiny particles called molecules. WIND is moving air molecules and pushes against anything in its path. The fabric and paper tied to the rope are in the wind's path and move when the moving air hits them. A lightweight material, especially if it has a large surface area, is easily moved by wind.

WIND CHIME

WIND

MATERIALS:
variety of metal objects such as –
  nuts, bolts, washers, screws, nails, car parts, jar lids
string
dowel or stick
outdoor area with tree

ART EXPERIMENT:
1. Tie a piece of string to one end of the stick, and another piece of string to the other end of the stick. These two strings will be used to hang the wind chime from a tree branch.
2. Tie pieces of string to each metal object.
3. Next, tie the strings to the stick so objects hang and bump into each other.
4. Carry the stick with the strings and metal objects outside to a tree and hang the stick with two pieces of string to a branch.
5. When the wind blows, the metal objects will bump into each other and make noises or chimes.

VARIATIONS:
*   Tie metal pipes with string to a stick or dowel. Pipes are hollow and make lovely chimes.
*   Hang shells, pieces of driftwood, and other items from nature on a larger stick or branch.

WIND is moving air molecules that push against the objects hanging from the stick and make them swing and bump into each other. GRAVITY causes each metal object to hang down from the stick on a string so that when the wind pushes the object one way, gravity pulls it back towards the earth. The string keeps the object from falling to the ground, and the object then swings the other way, again pulled back down by gravity and hit again by the wind. The objects swing back and forth in the wind, creating sounds when the metal objects collide.

LIGHT AND SIGHT
chapter 2

SPINNING DESIGNS

OPTICS

MATERIALS:
paper plates
pencil or scissors to punch hole in plate
pens or crayons
old record player

ART EXPERIMENT:
1. Draw any pattern or design on the paper plate or use one of the ideas shown on this page.
2. Punch a hole in the center of the paper plate with the end of the scissors or the pencil.
3. Place the plate on the record player and turn it on. (Do not use the arm and needle.)
4. Watch what happens to the pattern or design as the plate spins.

VARIATIONS:
- Make more patterns. Experiment with simple ones and very bold ones.
- Use tools such as a protractor, compass, or ruler to make designs.
- Place a blank paper plate on the record player. Draw on the plate with felt pens while it spins.

When designs or shapes on the paper plate spin, the visual process of the eye and brain combine the spinning IMAGES into a new shape or pattern. The brain continues to see overlapping images which appear to change shape or become one new shape.

HIDDEN COLORING

MATERIALS:

crayons
paper
shoe box
scissors

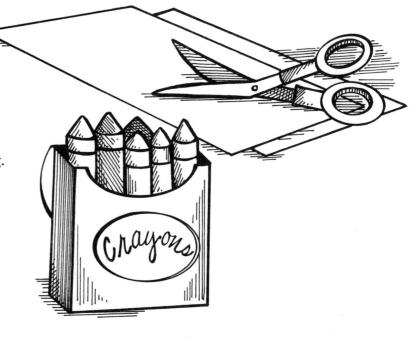

ART EXPERIMENT:

1. Use the scissors to cut a hole large enough to put a hand inside the shoe box.
2. Place a sheet of paper in the bottom of the box.
3. Draw on the paper inside the box without looking at the drawing.
4. Remove the drawing and see the results.

VARIATIONS:

- Write words, names, or messages inside the box without looking.
- Play a game where one person puts an object in the box, and the other person guesses what the object is just by feeling.

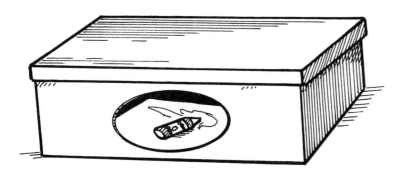

> *The coordination of the hand and the eye are connected through the brain. Sighted people depend on their VISION to control the movement of their hands. When vision is taken away, it is difficult to make the hands do what they should, but it is fun to try.*

SECRET PICTURES

OPTICS

MATERIALS:
lemon juice
cup
paintbrush
white bond paper
iron
newspaper

◆ adult help

ART EXPERIMENT:
1. Squeeze the juice of one lemon in a cup.
2. Dip a paintbrush in the lemon juice and paint on the white bond paper.
3. Let the picture dry thoroughly.
4. An adult can place the drawing between newspaper and iron it until a brown design appears.

VARIATIONS:
• Paint a Secret Picture for a friend or family member. Let them brown the picture with an iron for a surprise.
• Use Secret Pictures to write a secret message or give clues to a hidden treasure.

 When a picture is painted with lemon juice, it dries to an INVISIBLE design. Then when the electric iron heats the lemon juice markings, the natural sugar in the juice burns and becomes a brown carbon substance. This burned, browned juice is then seen as the secret painting or picture.

STRETCH PICTURE

MATERIALS:
magazine picture
scissors
glue
paper

ART EXPERIMENT:
1. Cut a magazine picture into four strips.
2. Arrange the picture on the paper leaving space between each strip.
3. Glue the strips onto the paper. See how the picture has stretched and how it makes the eyes feel to look at the stretched picture.

VARIATIONS:
- Cut a picture in more than four strips.
- Cut the picture in wavy or jagged strips.
- Cut a hand drawn picture instead of using a magazine picture.
- Use one piece of colored paper to cut out a shape instead of a magazine picture. Cut it into strips or pieces and "stretch" the shape. Glue the pieces on another piece of colored paper.

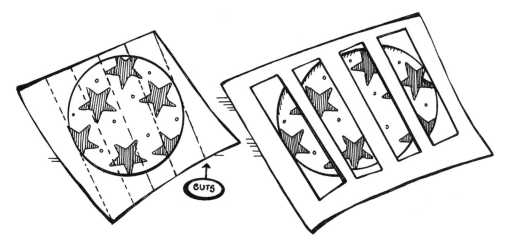

A Stretch Picture is an OPTICAL ILLUSION or a trick the eyes play on the brain. The eyes are not accustomed to seeing a picture that is cut into curvy strips or strips cut and spaced apart. The brain receives this unusual image and tries to make sense out of it by "filling in the gaps" in the picture and trying to make it seem more like a normal picture. The brain may even think the Stretch Picture seems to be moving or wiggling when it is really holding still.

DOT MATRIX PICTURE

OPTICS

MATERIALS:
strong magnifying glass
cotton swabs
several colors of tempera paints in jar lids
white drawing paper
dot matrix pictures from magazine or comic book

ART EXPERIMENT:
1. Look at the tiny dots in the dot matrix picture by using a strong magnifying glass.
2. Dip a cotton swab in the lids filled with tempera paint to make a dot matrix picture.
3. Then dab the swab on the paper by making many tiny dots and dabs to produce a picture. Use several colors. The dots will be a design or a picture when finished.

VARIATION:
- Imitate the famous impressionist and pointillism artist Georges Seurat by painting entire scenes with dots or dabs of paint only.

The comics and funny papers are good examples of dot matrix pictures. The dots are so small that they can't be easily seen, but the brain combines the dots and sees new colors created by the mixing of only a few colors of dots. Creating a dot matrix picture is similar to a painting technique called POINTILLISM *where paint is applied to the paper in small dots or points only; no lines are used.*

FACE ILLUSIONS

MATERIALS:
paper
crayons

ART EXPERIMENT:
1. Make a small dot in the center of the paper.
2. On one side of the dot, draw the outline of a face and color in a solid facial color.
3. On the other side of the dot, draw only the features of the face.
4. Hold the picture out at arms length and look at the dot.
5. Next, bring the paper closer and closer to the eyes while continuing to stare at the dot. The two drawings should seem to join into one drawing.

VARIATION:
- Create other combinations of two images on either side of the dot such as:
  - moon with craters, shadows, rocks
  - flower with bright tropical colors
  - map with rivers, roads, features
  - any shapes with colorful designs

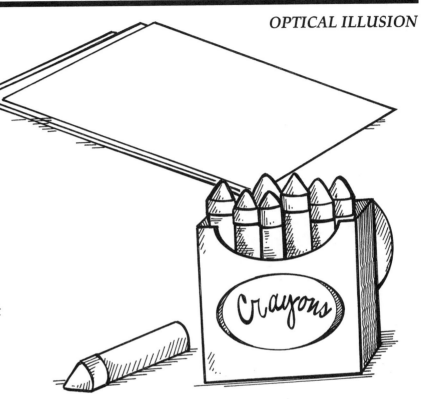

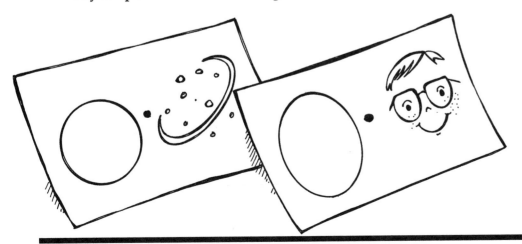

> *Human vision is* BINOCULAR *which means that light enters through two eyes. When two images like the outline of the face and the facial features enter both eyes, only one image is seen. If the drawing is too close to the eyes, the two drawings seem to become one blurred drawing, image stacked on image. This* OPTICAL ILLUSION *is like a trick played on the brain by the eyes.*

TISSUE COLOR MIX

PIGMENTS

MATERIALS:
colored art tissue paper (yellow, magenta, and bright blue)
scissors
liquid starch
paintbrush
white paper
water for rinsing

ART EXPERIMENT:
1. Cut art tissue into a variety of shapes.
2. Dip a paintbrush into liquid starch and use like glue to paint and stick tissue shapes to white paper.
3. Overlap shapes to create new colors. Rinse the brush in clear water between painting over the tissue paper colors. This will keep the colors bright.

VARIATIONS:
- Layer the following colored tissues to make new colors:
  - magenta over yellow to create red
  - bright blue over yellow to create green
  - magenta over bright blue to create purple
  - combinations of all three to create black
- Use starch to brush tissue pieces on clear plastic wrap. Then dry and tape the picture to a sunny window.
- Use liquid starch to "glue" tissue pieces to waxed paper.

The color in art tissue paper is made of chemical dyes called PIGMENTS. Each pigment takes in some kinds of light and gives off other kinds of light. This is why things are seen in color. When different colors of tissue papers are mixed or layered with the liquid starch, they combine and create a new color.

WHITE COLOR WHEEL

MATERIALS:
white cardboard or paper plate
cereal bowl or coffee can lid
scissors
paints (red, orange, yellow, green, cobalt blue, indigo, violet)
paintbrush
pencil
protractor or ruler

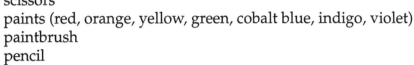

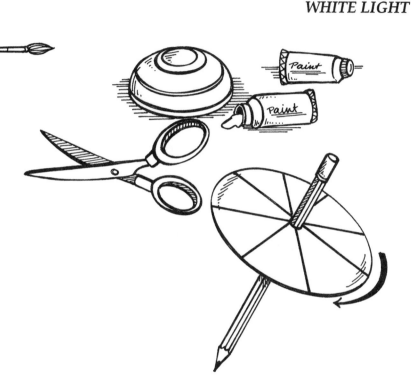

ART EXPERIMENT:
1. Draw a circle on the white cardboard by tracing a cereal bowl or coffee can lid.
2. Cut out the circle.
3. Draw seven sections on the circle using a protractor or ruler. Try to make them the same size. (This is the most fun of all!) Help may be needed.
4. Paint a different color on each section of the circle. Use red, green, yellow, orange, blue, indigo and violet.
5. Poke a hole in the middle of the circle to fit on a pencil.
6. Spin the color circle on the pencil.
7. Keep it spinning and watch the colors disappear as white is created.

VARIATIONS:
- Make a circle with only three colors and see what new color is made when the circle spins.
- Make a circle with any choice of colors and see what new color is made when the circle spins.

> *When mixing the rainbow colors of light (red, orange, yellow, green, blue, indigo, and violet), the result is WHITE LIGHT, just like from the sun. When the wheel spins, the eyes cannot keep up with the separate colored pie shapes, so the colors appear to blend. When the wheel spins it will look pale-gray unless perfectly pure colors were used in a perfectly correct balance. Pure white light is almost impossible to create but the White Color Wheel comes very close.*

SEE IT CARDS

REFLECTION

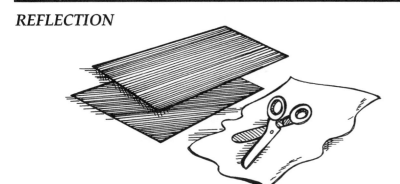

MATERIALS:
aluminum foil
dark colored cardboard cut into 6"x 6" (15 cm x 15 cm) cards
glue
scissors
sunny, outdoor area or bright light

ART EXPERIMENT:
1. Cut the aluminum foil into different shapes and patterns keeping the foil fairly smooth.
2. Glue the aluminum shapes shiny side up and close together on the dark cardboard.
3. Take the card outside or put it under a bright light to see the light reflect off the foil and onto other surfaces.

VARIATIONS:
- Go outside at night and shine a flashlight on the foil cards, reflecting the designs onto a wall or door.
- Reflect the shapes into a mirror.

> *The aluminum foil shapes are excellent REFLECTORS because foil is smooth and shiny, almost like a mirror. Light that hits the foil will bounce back or REFLECT, sometimes bouncing onto another surface like a wall where the foil reflection can be seen.*

SHADOW TIME

TIME

MATERIALS:
permanent marking pens or crayons
flower pot
stick (twice as tall as flower pot)
black marking pen or crayon
sunny day outdoors

ART EXPERIMENT:
1. Draw designs on the flower pot with permanent marking pens or crayons.
2. Turn the pot upside down and push a stick through the hole in the pot and into the ground.
    Important: Be sure the pot is in the sun.
3. At each hour, watch the shadow cast by the stick. Mark the shadow with a permanent marker or crayon on the bottom of the pot.
4. If the sun shines all day, there will be twelve marked shadows on the bottom of the pot, one for each of the twelve hours.

VARIATION:
• Tie a long string (about 3 ft. or 1 m) to a tall stick in the middle of the yard. Each hour, move the loose end of the string in line with the shadow made by the tall stick. Mark this shadow by placing a shorter stick in the ground at the loose end of the string (but do not tie the string to the stick). After twelve hours, there will be a semi-circle of sticks in the yard around the tall center stick. The next sunny day, watch where the shadow falls and tell the time by the hour.

The earth turns or ROTATES *once each day which makes day and night. Ancient people used a* SUNDIAL *to measure the turning or rotating of the earth each hour and to keep track of* TIME. *By watching the shadow made by the sun with the stick during the day and marking its movement each hour, the turning of the earth can be measured.*

INFINITY REFLECTION

REFLECTION

MATERIALS:
2 mirrors
person to look in mirror
colorful shapes glued to cardboard cards

◆ adult help

ART EXPERIMENT:
1. Set up two facing mirrors so that they are almost parallel. (see illustration)
2. Stand between them and look into the mirrors.
3. Observe the infinite images.
4. Next, hold one of the colorful shape cardboards up to the mirrors.
5. Adjust and experiment with the shapes to achieve different infinite designs.

VARIATIONS:
• Hold other objects, paintings, and shapes up to the mirrors to experiment with infinite designs.
• Count the number of infinite images seen.

A mirror is a smooth, shiny surface called a REFLECTOR which means that light hitting the mirror will bounce off. When two mirrors are facing each other, the light from the person bounces off one mirror and onto the other mirror. The light will keep bouncing or REFLECTING from mirror to mirror, back and forth, creating many, many images of one person. Holding colorful cards up to the double mirrors will create endless reflections of designs.

MIRROR PAINTING

MATERIALS:
hand mirror
tempera paints
paintbrushes
table
newspaper

ART EXPERIMENT:
1. Spread newspaper on the table.
2. Lay the hand mirror on the newspaper.
3. Look into the mirror.
4. Use tempera paints and brushes to paint a face and features on the mirror.
   Note: The mirror can be washed with warm soapy water, dried, and used again.

VARIATIONS:
- Paint a hat, beard, jewelry, or unusual hair on the person in the mirror.
- Use a full-length mirror to paint the entire body.
- Paint any design on the mirror to enjoy the slippery surface.
- Draw with water-based marking pens on the mirror.

When looking in a mirror, the light from that face bounces back to the eyes and a REFLECTION is seen. A mirror is a perfect REFLECTOR because all light that hits a mirror bounces off. To be a good reflector, the material must be very smooth and shiny, just like a mirror.

OPAQUE

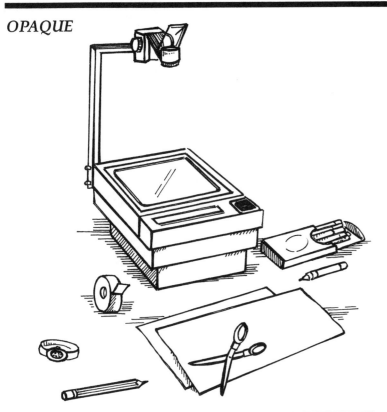

MATERIALS:
overhead projector
objects like scissors, pen, wrist watch
large paper
wall
colored markers
masking tape

ART EXPERIMENT:
1. Set up the overhead projector away from the wall.
2. Place several objects on the overhead.
3. Turn the overhead on so it shines on the wall. Move the projector and focus so objects have clear edges.
4. Tape the paper on the wall so the objects flash on the paper.
5. Trace around the shapes of the objects on the paper.
6. Then turn off the overhead.
7. Remove the paper from the wall to the floor. Fill in, color, paint, or decorate and design the traced objects to be realistic or imaginary.

VARIATIONS:
• Use plastic or cut-out letters to spell words.
• Use geometric shapes and make patterns or designs.
• Experiment with transparent objects such as shapes cut from clear or almost clear plastic bottles.

A solid object that blocks all light is called OPAQUE *because light cannot pass through the object. The light from the overhead projector shines up, hits a mirror, and is* REFLECTED *onto the wall. When a solid or* OPAQUE *object like the scissors is placed on the projector's glass table, a shadow is created on the wall the exact shape of the scissors. The shadow will be larger than the actual object because the light beam from the projector spreads out slightly as it travels to the wall.*

COLOR AND SHINE

MATERIALS:
transparency film
overhead projector
colored markers
darkened room

TRANSLUCENT

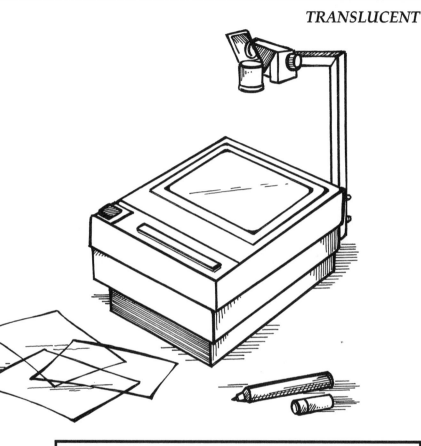

ART EXPERIMENT:
1. Draw on the transparency film with colored markers.
2. Place the transparency film on the projector.
3. Show the drawing on the wall.

VARIATIONS:
- Use a variety of paints and other types of markers to find which are transparent.
- Cut colored tissues and cellophanes in shapes and place them in designs on the overhead projector.

> The overhead projector uses a strong light and mirrors to REFLECT the drawing made by the colored markers onto the wall. The colored markings are TRANSLUCENT, which means light from the projector can pass through the markings. The light beam spreads out as it travels from the project to the wall making the drawing on the wall larger than the drawing on the transparency film.

SLIDE VIEWER

TRANSLUCENT

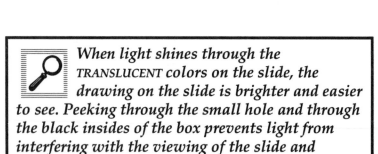

MATERIALS:
small box (about 4" x 1-1/2" or 10 cm x 4 cm) with lid
black paint and paintbrush
tape
scissors
plastic transparency sheet
felt pens (pens for drawing on plastic work best)

ART EXPERIMENT:
1. Remove one small end of the box.
2. Paint the inside of the box black. Dry.
3. Poke a small peek-hole in the other end of the box (about 1/8" or .3 cm).
4. Mark a square on the transparency sheet about 1-1/2" (4 cm) square.
5. Draw a design in the square with felt pens.
6. Cut out the square design and tape it over the open end of the box.
7. Hold the box up to the light and peek through the tiny hole to view the slide.

VARIATIONS:
• Use real processed slides.
• Use slides of the child who is doing the project.
• Use slides that go with a theme or study area.
• Draw large slides to view through a large box.

> *When light shines through the* TRANSLUCENT *colors on the slide, the drawing on the slide is brighter and easier to see. Peeking through the small hole and through the black insides of the box prevents light from interfering with the viewing of the slide and reduces glare.*

SLIDE SHOW

TRANSLUCENT

MATERIALS:
old slides
slide projector
bleach
fine point permanent markers
cotton swabs

◆ adult help

ART EXPERIMENT:
1. Adult prepare the slides –
   Dip a cotton swab into the bleach and clean all color and image from the slide until clear. Let dry.
2. Draw with permanent fine point markers on each slide.
   Draw colorful designs or realistic drawings.
3. Place completed slides in a slide projector and show on a blank wall or on a screen.

VARIATIONS:
• Add music to the Slide Show.
• Design slides that tell a story or interpret a poem or song. Tell the story, say the poem, or sing the song along with the Slide Show.

The colors drawn on the slide with pen are TRANSLUCENT which means that some light, but not all, can pass through the drawing. The light beam that shines through the slide spreads out as it travels to the wall. When the light hits the wall it is REFLECTED or bounced back to the eyes. An enlarged but identical picture can be seen reflected on the wall.

SILHOUETTES

OPAQUE

MATERIALS:
slide projector
blank wall
tape
white crayon
person
chair
scissors
black paper
white paper

◆ adult help

ART EXPERIMENT:
1. Place the slide projector on a table several feet away from a blank wall.
2. Turn on the projector.
3. Place a chair next to the wall.
4. Have a person sit sideways on the chair so the profile can be seen.
5. Tape black paper on the wall so the profile falls on the paper.
6. Trace around the profile with a white crayon.
7. When complete, cut out the traced shape on the white line which will be the silhouette.
8. Spread glue on the crayon side of the black silhouette and stick to a sheet of white paper.

VARIATIONS:
• Set objects on the chair such as a stuffed animal, statue, or a vase of flowers. Trace the silhouette of the object, cut out, and glue on white paper.
• Make Silhouettes with other colors of paper.

Light travels in a straight path. The light from the slide projector cannot curve around the person on the chair or pass through the person. The person is OPAQUE *and blocks the light, casting a* SHADOW *on the wall. The shadow is basically the same shape as the person, but may be bigger or smaller depending on the angle of light hitting the person and the distance the person is from the wall. The shadow which occurs on the wall is called a* SILHOUETTE.

SILHOUETTE SHOW

MATERIALS:
slide projector (or lamp without shade)
table
blank wall
chair or chairs
craft sticks or straws
paper
tape
scissors

ART EXPERIMENT:
1. Draw outlines of characters, people, animals, or scenery such as houses and trees on any paper. Cut outlines out with scissors. The cut-outs are silhouttes.
2. Tape the silhouette cut-outs to a craft stick or drinking straw.
3. Set up the slide projector or lamp near a wall. Turn on the projector or lamp so the light shines on the blank wall.
4. Place several chairs by the light on the wall. (Be cautious of electric cord from projector or lamp.)
5. While sitting on chairs with backs to the light, hold up silhouette cut-outs so their shadows show on the wall.
6. Perform a Silhouette Show on the wall. (Several people may be needed for holding the silhouettes.)

VARIATIONS:
- Act out a favorite story, nursery rhyme, or tale.
- Make up stories to act out.
- Use real objects instead of cut-outs for the silhouettes.

OPAQUE

Light from the slide projector travels in a straight line. When it hits the cut-out paper characters, it cannot curve around them or pass through them because the paper is OPAQUE. *A* SHADOW *is created on the wall which is basically the same shape as the opaque paper cut-out that blocks the light. Another name for the shadow on the wall is a* SILHOUETTE.

FLASHLIGHT PATTERNS

OPAQUE

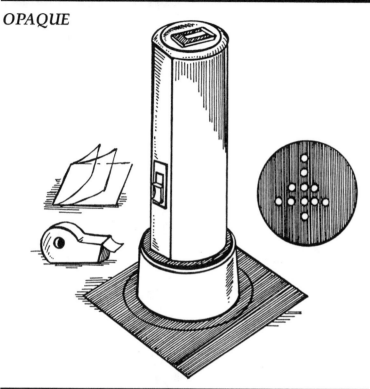

MATERIALS:
flashlight
black construction paper
colored cellophane
scissors
pencils
masking tape
paper punch

ART EXPERIMENT:
1. Stand the flashlight on the black paper with the light side down.
2. Use the pencil to draw a circle about 1/2" (1-1/4 cm) larger than the lens of the flashlight.
3. Remove the flashlight and cut out the circle.
4. Next punch several holes in the circle to make a pattern.
5. Put the circle with the holes over the flashlight lens and tape around the edges.
6. Now tape cellophane over the circle.
7. In a dark room, shine the flashlight on the ceiling to see the colored pattern made by the cellophane and circle.

VARIATIONS:
• Cut other designs, letters, or shapes out of black paper circles and shine their patterns on the wall or ceiling.
• Cover the lens of a flashlight with plastic wrap held in place with a rubber band to see the unusual pattern made.
• Experiment with other transparent materials.

Materials can be OPAQUE, TRANSLUCENT or TRANSPARENT. TRANSPARENT materials are clear like the glass of the flashlight lens and allow all light to pass through them. TRANSLUCENT materials, like the colored cellophane, allow some light to shine through them, but not all. OPAQUE materials, like the black construction paper, block all light and no light shines through them. When the flashlight's beam of light shines through the TRANSLUCENT cellophane, but not through the OPAQUE black paper, colored designs are created on the ceiling.

FLASHLIGHT REFLECTIONS

MATERIALS:
flashlight
small flat mirror
white cardboard
other colors of paper
crayons or pens
scissors
piece of tape

◆ adult help

ART EXPERIMENT:
1. Hold up the mirror and the white card at a right angle to each other.
2. Turn out the lights so the room is darkened.
3. Shine the flashlight onto the mirror.
   (The light will reflect onto the card.)
4. Now cut a circle of paper to fit over the lens of the flashlight. Then cut a design in the middle of this circle.
5. Next, stick the circle design to the flashlight lens with a piece of tape.
6. Repeat steps 1 through 3, shining the light onto the mirror which reflects onto the card and observe the reflection of the design taped over the flashlight.

VARIATIONS:
• Experiment with the results of different designs and also different colors of cards other than white.
• Try covering the card with aluminum foil.
• Try using a mirror in place of the white card so that one mirror reflects into a second mirror.

 A mirror has a smooth, shiny backing and surface. The light that hits the mirror bounces off or REFLECTS. *Light bouncing off a mirror is called* REFLECTION, *just like a ball bouncing off a wall. The light design bounces off the mirror and onto the white card.*

COLOR VIEWING BOX

FILTER

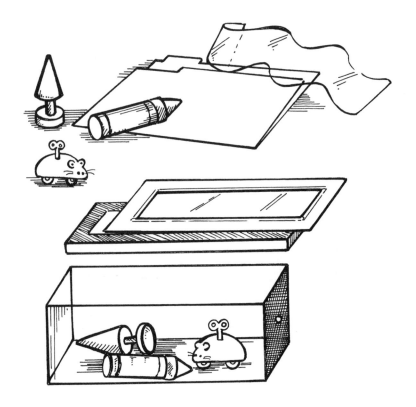

MATERIALS:
old file folders
shoe box and lid
colored cellophane or art tissue
tape
colorful small objects, such as small toys
scissors

ART EXPERIMENT:
1. Cut old file folders into cards about the same size as the shoe box lid. Make several cards this size.
2. Cut a large hole in the lid and also in the cards, being sure to leave about 2" (5 cm) around all of the sides. This will resemble a picture frame.
3. Tape different colors of cellophane or art tissue to the card frames.
4. Cut a small hole in one end of the shoe box.
5. Put colorful objects inside the box.
6. Place the colored cards over the top of the shoe box and view the colors of the objects inside.
   (Hint: It helps to have a strong light to shine through the colored cards and into the box.)

VARIATIONS:
- Walk about looking through a colored frame and see the world. See how colors change while walking.
- Cover old sunglasses (without lenses) with cellophane. Wear and observe the world through colored lenses.
- Draw characters from a favorite story and glue them inside the box to make a scene.
- Construct a winter scene in the box and use a blue color frame.
- Construct a summer scene in the box and use a yellow color frame.

Looking through colored pieces of cellophane changes the way the objects in the box look. The colored cellophane is a FILTER. When looking through red cellophane, a blue crayon in the box will no longer look blue. This is because the cellophane lets some of the light through but filters out the rest.

REAL CAMERA

MATERIALS:
shoe box
pin
black paint
paintbrush
sheet of photographic film (not exposed to light)
completely darkened room with no light
masking tape

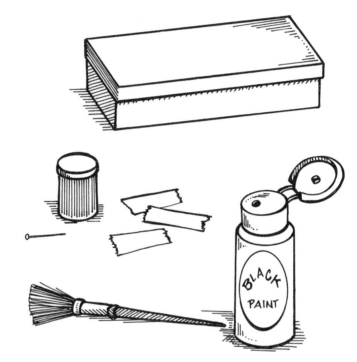

ART EXPERIMENT:
1. Paint the inside of the box and lid black.
2. Make a pinhole in the center of one end of the box and put masking tape over the hole.
3. Switch the lights off and make sure the room is completely dark.
4. In the dark, tape a piece of the film on the end of the inside wall of the box directly opposite the pinhole. The dull side of the film should face the pinhole.
5. Still working in the dark, put the lid on the box and tape around it. No light must get into the box.
6. The camera is now ready. Place the camera on the table with the pinhole facing the window. Place something in front of the window to take a picture of.
7. Being careful not to move the box, peel off the masking tape and leave the camera for 15 minutes.
8. Restick the tape carefully and, in the dark, remove the film and put it back in its envelope. Turn the light back on.
9. Take the film to a photo processing business to be developed.

The hole in the box acts like the LENS of a camera. The light from the window scene comes into the hole from many different angles traveling in straight lines. As the light from the window passes through the hole, it continues on until it hits the film. The film reacts to the light and reproduces a smaller version of the window scene on its surface. Too much light would expose the film and no image would be captured.

STAR WINDOW

MATERIALS:
clear night outdoors
newspapers
black construction paper
items to poke holes –
    scissors
    pin
    nail
    pencil
window
tape

ART EXPERIMENT:
1. Look at stars on a clear night. Notice the different sizes of the dots of light in the sky and the patterns they seem to form.
2. Go inside. Place a piece black paper on a thick pad of newspaper.
3. Poke holes of different sizes through the black paper, copying the stars seen in the sky or creating patterns and stars from the imagination. Use the scissors, pin, nail, and pencil to make different sizes of holes.
4. When finished, tape the corners of the black paper to a window. The light shining through the window during the day will make the stars and patterns visible.

VARIATIONS:
- Tape colored tissue or cellophane behind the holes to give the stars colors.
- Cut large holes or shapes and cover with colored tissue for a stained glass effect or a light design.
- With a white pencil or chalk, connect the "dots" and form pictures, patterns, or shapes.

> *Ancient and modern civilizations have always imagined objects, animals, and people in the patterns of stars in the sky which are called* CONSTELLATIONS. *Each constellation usually has an imaginative story or tale that goes along with it telling how that star pattern came to be. One of the most common constellations is The Big Dipper.*

WINDOW SCENE

MATERIALS:
colored tissue paper
plastic wrap
liquid starch in a cup
scissors
tape
paintbrush
table covered with newspaper

ART EXPERIMENT:
1. Cut a piece of plastic wrap to fit a window.
   (For big windows, pull out a piece any size desired.)
2. Tape the corners of the plastic wrap to the newspaper on the table.
3. Cut bits of colored art tissue into shapes, characters, pictures, or a scene.
4. Use a paintbrush to paint the starch over the plastic wrap.
5. Next, place colored tissue pieces into the starch on the plastic wrap.
6. Then paint over these colored tissue pieces with more starch. Keep adding tissue designs until finished.
7. Let the project dry completely (usually an hour or so).
8. Remove the tape or cut it at the corners of the plastic.
9. Tape the plastic wrap Window Scene to a window and watch the light shine through the translucent tissue.

VARIATIONS:
- Make a Window Scene on waxed paper with starch.
- Make a scene on white paper to display on the wall.
- Make a Window Scene by sticking tissue paper to clear contact paper; then cover the scene with another piece of clear contact paper to seal the design.
- Punch holes in the top of the window scene, lace yarn through the holes, and display in any lighted area.

> *Materials that block light are called* OPAQUE. *Materials that allow some light to pass through are called* TRANSLUCENT *like the tissues in Window Scene.*

BUBBLE SCULPTURE

REFLECTION

MATERIALS:
flexible, thin wire
strong dishwashing detergent (such as Dawn)
bucket half-filled with water
3 T. (45 ml) sugar

ART EXPERIMENT:
1. Take a piece of wire and bend it into any shape.
   Be sure to close the shape. (A circle, geometric shape, figures, or animals work well.)
2. Bend the top of the wire to make a hanger.
3. Add all the dishwashing soap to the bucket of water.
4. Add the 3 T. of sugar to make the solution thicker.
5. Dip the wire shape into the soap solution.
6. Pull the wire shape filled with bubble solution out slowly and look at the colors.
   (Find the colored bands in the bubbles. Observe any change as the soap runs to the bottom of the shape.)
7. Try blowing the solution into a bubble that floats away.
   (Observe the shapes of the bubbles as they float.)

VARIATIONS:
- Experiment making animal shapes from wire.
- Use a wire hanger to bend into a shape. Dip the hanger into a large tub of bubble solution.
- Experiment with other objects to find which ones will make bubbles, such as canning jar rings, toys, slotted spoons, or a clean flyswatter.

The colors on the soap bubble's surface are caused when light rays REFLECTING from the inner surface of the bubble interfere with light rays REFLECTING from the outer surface of the bubble. Some colors cancel out and disappear and other colors combine forming bands of color on the bubble's surface.

MOTION AND ENERGY
chapter 3

SHAKE PICTURE

ENERGY

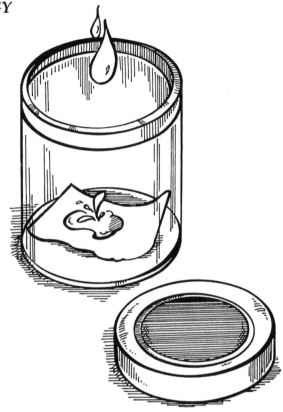

MATERIALS:
construction paper
scissors
liquid tempera paint
large jar with lid

ART EXPERIMENT:
1. Cut the paper small enough to fit inside the jar.
2. Put the paper in the jar as shown.
3. Put several drops of paint in the jar.
4. Put on the lid and shake the jar.
5. Open the jar and remove the Shake Picture.
6. Let the painting dry.

VARIATIONS:
- Repeat the above activity with two or more colors in one jar.
- After shaking one color in the jar, put the painting in a second jar and add a second color.
- Before painting, put small pieces of tape on the paper. After the painting dries, remove the tape for a stencil effect.

For every action there is a reaction. Shaking the jar causes the paint to react to the action of shaking and to interact with the paper. It takes ENERGY *from muscles to make the paint move around in the jar. Whenever the paint hits paper it will stick in random patterns because the paper is* ABSORBENT *which means the solid paper is soaking up the liquid paint.*

PAINT RACING

MATERIALS:
liquid tempera paint
board from easel, with paint tray attached
stack of blocks
marbles, toy cars, small balls, spools
long piece of butcher paper
newspaper

◆ adult help

ART EXPERIMENT:
1. Cover the easel board with butcher paper. Protect the floor with newspaper.
2. Make an incline with the board propped up on blocks, with the paint tray at the bottom of the incline (to catch rolling objects).
3. Dip one toy at a time, such as a marble or a toy car, in the paint in a jar lid or shallow cup.
4. Place the toy at the top of the inclined easel board and let it roll down making paint patterns.

VARIATIONS:
- Raise or lower the incline to change the speed of rolling or change designs made by toys.
- Push a toy dipped in paint down the incline to force patterns.
- Using a spoon or squeeze bottle of paint, place blobs of paint on the paper on the incline. Roll toys, one at a time, through the paint blobs.

> *Toy cars, marbles, and balls all roll down the inclined easel board because of the force of GRAVITY but are slowed down because of the force of FRICTION. Friction will slow the rolling toy or ball as the surface of the toy rubs against the paint on the paper. Gravity also keeps the toys from rolling "up." Changing the thickness of the paint will increase or decrease the friction of the rolling object making it faster or slower as it rolls across the paper. Experiment with gravity and friction by mixing different thicknesses of paint.*

STREAK SPIN

OPTICS

MATERIALS:
black construction paper
scissors
white chalk
pencil
masking tape

ART EXPERIMENT:
1. Cut a 6" (15 cm) diameter circle from the black paper.
2. Use chalk to place dots on the black circle.
3. Poke the pencil point through the center of the circle. Use masking tape to secure the circle to the pencil on the underside.
4. Twirl the pencil back and forth between the palms of the hands and watch the white dots appear to become streaks.

VARIATION:
- Draw many colors of dots on a white circle with crayons. Twirl between the hands.

The brain remembers the dots of chalk on the paper, but as the paper spins, the eye and the mind see rings on the paper because the eyes can't keep up with the spinning IMAGE of dots going around so quickly.

TWIRLING RAINBOW

MATERIALS:
small paper plate with edges trimmed away
pencil
masking tape
eyedropper
tempera paint, thinned
outdoor area
apron

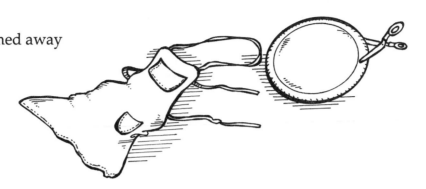

ART EXPERIMENT:
1. Do this activity outside and cover clothing with an apron before beginning.
2. Push the point of the pencil through the center of the paper plate circle. Secure the paper plate to the pencil with masking tape.
3. Place a drop of paint on top of the circle near the pencil.
4. Hold the pencil between the palms of the hands and twirl the pencil, spreading the paint swirling around the paper.

VARIATIONS:
• Cut different shapes and types of paper to spin on the pencil.
• Use thicker tempera paint.
• Use food coloring.

When drops of paint are twirled on the plate, the paint spins out and away from the pencil forming sunburst designs. The pencil is the AXIS and is the center of CENTRIFUGAL FORCE. The paint moves out from the axis in equal force from the center to the outside edge of the plate.

MOVING PETS

OPTICAL ILLUSION

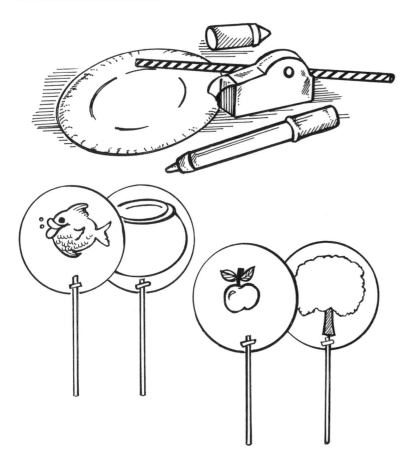

MATERIALS:
heavy paper, such as a paper plate
crayons or colored pens
dowel, pencil, or straw
tape

ART EXPERIMENT:
1. Think of a pet and where it lives such as:
   – a fish in a bowl
   – a dog in a dog house
   – a cat in a basket
   – a bird in a cage
2. Cut the rough edges of the paper plates off.
3. Draw a pet on one paper plate circle.
4. Draw the house or bed of the pet on the other paper plate circle.
5. Tape the circles to the dowel or pencil being careful not to cover the drawings with tape.
6. Hold the dowel or pencil between the palms of the hands and rub hands together to make the dowel twist quickly backwards and forwards. The pet will "appear" in its house or bed.

VARIATIONS:
- Draw any two items which go together such as:
   – a hotdog in a bun
   – a smile on a face
   – an apple in a tree
   – money in a bank

> *Two pictures moving very quickly in front of the eyes will appear to be one IMAGE. This phenomenon is called an OPTICAL ILLUSION. There are really two pictures, but the brain sees them as one because they are moving so quickly the eyes can't keep up with the movement.*

SPOKE WEAVING

MATERIALS:
tricycle
paper
ribbon, crepe paper, yarn
outdoor play area

ART EXPERIMENT:
1. Turn the tricycle on its side so the big wheel turns freely.
2. Create designs in the wheel weaving and tying the yarn, crepe paper, and ribbons in the spokes.
3. Spin the wheel to see the design. Be careful to keep fingers, loose hair and clothes away from the spinning wheel.
4. Decorate the two small wheels too. Spin all three wheels.

VARIATIONS:
- Decorate trikes and bikes and have a parade!
- Tie two colors of crepe paper, such as yellow and blue, in the spokes. Spin the wheel to see if the colors blend into a new color such as green.
- Decorate the spokes with an environmental theme such as twigs, leaves, flowers, and litter.

> *The decorated wheel on the tricycle spins very rapidly. The human eye can't keep up with the speeding* IMAGES *so the brain blends the colors and shapes together into a blur of moving, mixing colors and shapes. As the spinning wheel slows down, the eye can begin to see separate decorations and individual colors.*

MARBLE SCULPTURE

GRAVITY

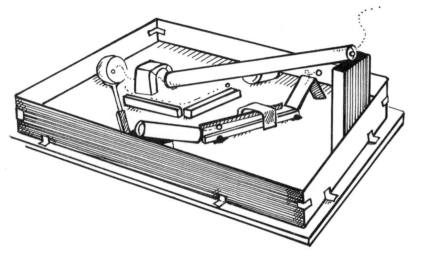

MATERIALS:
table
marbles
heavy paper strips
tape
scissors

sculpture materials –
    playdough
    pipe insulation
    plastic pipes
    baskets
    yogurt cups
    blocks
    cardboard tubes
    cans
    other materials

ART EXPERIMENT:
1. Tape paper strips around the edge of the table to keep the marbles from rolling off.
2. Place other sculpture materials on the table and begin building a sculpture for marbles to roll through, into, and over.
3. Use inclines and connecting tracks and tunnels for marbles to follow. Playdough can be used to support tubes, pipes, and cans for tunnels and tracks.
4. Send marbles through the sculpture.

VARIATIONS:
- In a box lid, draw a face. Instead of drawing eyeballs, punch or cut two holes where the eyeballs should be. Next, place two marbles in the lid. Tilt the lid back and forth, trying to put the marbles in the eye spaces.
- Invent other lid and marble games.

A marble is a smooth round object that rolls easily. Once the marble starts moving it will keep moving for a long time or until something stops it. This demonstrates a law of physics called INERTIA, which states that an object in motion will remain in motion. Other laws can get in the way of the rolling marble like those of GRAVITY and FRICTION. Gravity is the force that pulls all things toward the earth and causes the marble to roll down the inclined ramps. Friction is the rubbing together of materials like the marble against any surface which slows the marble down.

GEAR SCULPTURE

GEARS

MATERIALS:
jar lids of various sizes
empty thread spools
glue
thick cardboard
two 1-1/2" nails, more nails optional
sandpaper cut into strips for edges of lids

◆ adult help

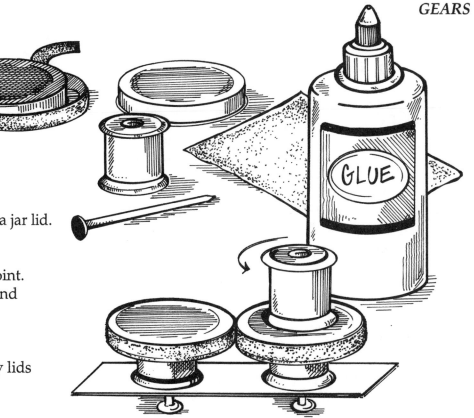

ART EXPERIMENT:
1. Push a nail up through the cardboard to make an axle for a jar lid.
2. Glue strips of sandpaper to the edges of two lids.
3. Next, glue empty spools under the same lids.
4. Slip the hole of a spool with a lid attached over the nail point.
5. Push another nail through the cardboard so a second lid and spool will touch the first lid and spool.
6. Glue a spool to one lid top to be used as a handle.
7. Turn this handle lid so the other lid turns too.
8. Add lids with sandpaper edges and nail axle so that many lids will touch and turn.

VARIATIONS:
- Adjust the colors of the lids and spools for a lively moving sculpture.
- Lids can be decorated by gluing a circle of paper that has been colored or painted to the top of the lid.
- Use larger and smaller lids in a series to create a connection of moving discs.

> *The rough surface of the sandpaper will not slide easily because the grains of sand catch on each other. This is similar to the teeth on a real GEAR. The turning motion of one gear is transferred to the next gear that is turned in the opposite direction. By moving only one lid, many other lids will move if each lid touches the next. In this way, a lot of work can be done by turning only one lid.*

PAINT PENDULUM

GRAVITY

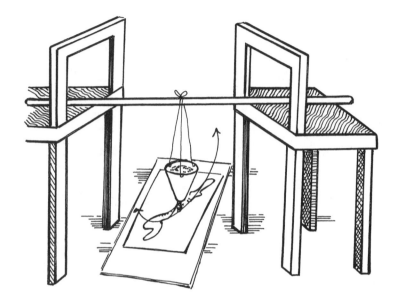

> A PENDULUM *is a hanging object that swings freely because of the force of* GRAVITY. *Gravity is the force that pulls things down to the center of the earth. To swing a pendulum, an object is lifted up and then released.* GRAVITY *tries to pull the object down to the earth, but the string prevents it from falling straight down. Instead, the weight swings back and forth, until the force of gravity overcomes the inertia created by the swinging cup. As the paint dribbles out of the cup, the pendulum paints a design caused by gravity and motion.*

MATERIALS:
paper cup (preferably cone shaped)
string
scissors
dowel rod
two chairs
tempera paints, thinned until runny
newspaper
masking tape
construction paper

◆ adult help

ART EXPERIMENT:
1. Poke three holes in the top of the cup using the scissors point.
2. Lace string through the holes, gather the strings, and tie them in a knot above the cup.
3. Tie the cup with the string to the center of the dowel rod.
4. With the two chairs spaced apart and back to back, place the dowel rod on the seats of the chairs so the cup can swing freely.
5. Cover the floor under the cup with newspaper. Then place a sheet of construction paper on top of the newspaper.
6. Poke a tiny hole in the point of the cup so that paint can flow through it slowly.
7. Then put masking tape over the hole.
8. Pour runny tempera paint into the cup until it is half full.
9. Pull the tape off and swing the cup slowly over the paper releasing the paint and letting the cup swing freely.
10. Add more paint and continue making the pendulum painting until complete.

SALT PENDULUM

MATERIALS:

sharp pencil
broomstick or dowel
string
box of salt
large sheet of black paper

two matching chairs
paper cup
scissors
masking tape
newspaper

◆ adult help

ART EXPERIMENT:

1. With the sharp pencil, punch a small hole in the center of the bottom of a paper cup. (Hint: punch from the inside out...adult help recommended.)
2. Make three holes in the rim of the cup, Spaced evenly apart.
3. Cut three pieces of string, and run them through the three holes. Tie the three ends into a knot as shown.
4. Set up two matching chairs back to back and apart with the broomstick between the top of both chair backs. Tape the broomstick to the backs to secure.
5. Cut a long piece of string (long enough to reach from the broomstick to the floor.)
6. Tie one end of this long string to the broom and the other end to the knot in the cup's string.
7. Cover the floor with newspaper to catch spills.
8. Lay the black paper on top of the newspaper beneath the cup.
9. Cover the hole in the cup with one finger and fill the cup with salt.
10. Swing the pendulum and let go of the salt hole.
11. As the salt pours from the cup, it will mark a pattern of movement on the black paper.

> A PENDULUM *is a hanging object that swings freely because of the force of* GRAVITY. *Gravity is the force that pulls things down to the center of the earth. To swing a pendulum, an object is lifted up and then released.* GRAVITY *tries to pull the object down to the earth, but the string prevents it from falling straight down. Instead, the weight swings back and forth. As the salt dribbles out of the cup, the pendulum draws a design caused by gravity and resulting swinging motion.*

POLISHED CRAYON

MELTING / FRICTION

MATERIALS:
crayons
paper towels
paper

ART EXPERIMENT:
1. Press hard with a crayon to draw a picture or design on the paper. (Use lots of bright crayon, coloring hard.)
2. Place the paper towel over a pointer finger and polish the crayon marks until they smear together, blend, and shine.

VARIATIONS:
- Color with crayon on a sheet of paper. Then polish the marks. Next add chalk to the crayon drawing and smear both of these to blend chalk and crayon.
- Place paper on a warm surface, such as a buffet warming tray. Draw on warm paper with old crayons (paper peeled).

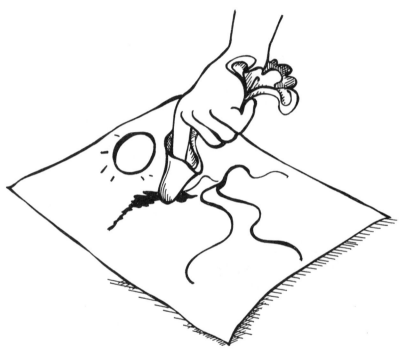

When the crayon drawing is rubbed vigorously, heat is created from the FRICTION. *The wax molecules move faster and spread out or* MELT. *When the friction stops, the crayon wax cools and the molecules slow down and hold the new, smoother shape caused by friction.*

CRAYON CREATURES

MELTING

MATERIALS:
cookie cutters in a variety of animal or character shapes
heavy duty aluminum foil
peeled, broken crayon stubs
cookie sheet
oven
yarn or ribbon, optional

◆ adult help

– developed by Amy Cheney of Bellingham, WA, age 10,
whose hands are shown on the back cover of this book

ART EXPERIMENT:
1. Cover the bottom of each cookie cutter with two layers of heavy duty foil to prevent leaking of melted crayon.
2. Place the foiled cookie cutters on a cookie sheet.
3. Fill each cookie cutter with peeled, broken crayon stubs. (Mix colors for a rainbow effect or fill with one color for a single color result.)
4. Place the cookie sheet in a warm oven for about 10 minutes or until crayon stubs melt a little and float but are not totally liquid.
5. Next, place the entire cookie sheet with cookie cutters into the freezer for about 1/2 hour.
6. Remove crayon creatures from the freezer and then from cookie cutters carefully.
7. Tie a ribbon around each creature's neck if desired.
8. Color with Crayon Creatures like crayons.
9. Cookie cutters will need hot, soapy water to clean.

VARIATIONS:
• Use other shapes of cookie cutters such as circles, trees, or stars. Follow melting and freezing directions. Use for gifts, holiday decorations, or just coloring.
• Use Crayon Creatures for crayon rubbings.

> *To MELT the crayons they must be heated. When heated, the molecules in the crayons move faster and spread apart which allows the crayon materials to flow and fill the shape of the cookie cutter mold. Cooling returns the molecules to their solid state and the crayons continue to hold the new shape of the mold.*

HOT SANDPAPER

MELTING

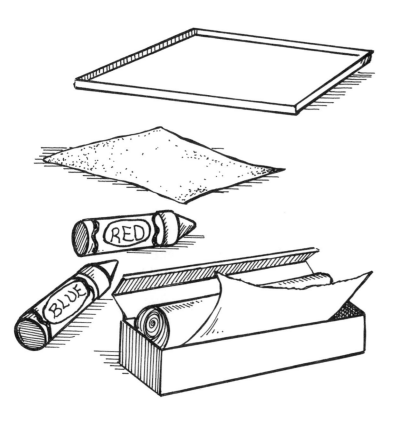

MATERIALS:
fine sandpaper
crayons
low oven, about 250°F (120°C)
aluminum foil
cookie sheet

◆ adult help

ART EXPERIMENT:
1. Line the cookie sheet with the foil.
2. Draw on the sandpaper pressing hard with the crayons.
3. Put the sandpaper drawing on the foil.
4. Bake the drawing for 10 to 15 seconds at 250°F (120°C) to slowly melt the crayon drawing.

VARIATIONS:
- While the sandpaper drawing is still warm and soft, press a piece of white typing paper over the design. Then peel off the paper for a sandpaper print.
- Drop bits of crayon shavings or crayon stubs on a foil covered cookie sheet. Melt in a warm oven. Remove this from the oven. Press a piece of paper over the melted crayon and then peel off for a print.

Every material has a MELTING POINT, the temperature at which a material changes from solid to liquid. The melting point of crayon is very low and occurs easily in a warm oven. The melting crayon flows and spreads over the sandpaper and then hardens to a solid again when cooled.

BAKED DRAWINGS

MATERIALS:

crayon
cardboard or heavy paper
warm oven
cookie sheet
aluminum foil

◆ adult help

ART EXPERIMENT:
1. Draw a design on the heavy paper or cardboard. (Matte board scraps from frame shops work well.)
2. Color and press hard with crayons so the colors are bright and applied in a heavy coat.
3. When finished, place the drawing on a foil covered cookie sheet.
4. Put the cookie sheet and drawing in the warm oven with the door open and watch the drawing melt.
5. Carefully remove the picture when melted. Cool.

VARIATIONS:
• Draw on a rock with crayon and melt the markings on the rock in a low, warm oven.
• Draw on sand paper and melt in a low, warm oven.
• Experiment with other papers and materials drawn on with crayon and warmed in the oven.

Every material has a MELTING POINT, *the temperature at which the material will change from a solid to a liquid. The melting point of the wax in crayons is very low and occurs easily in a warm oven. The crayon wax flows over the paper when it is a liquid and then hardens to a solid again when it is cooled.*

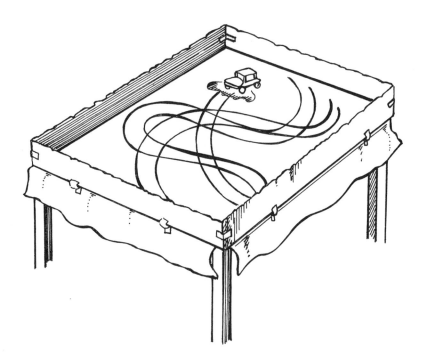

MOTOR CAR PRINT

ELECTRICITY

MATERIALS:
small battery operated toy car
table covered with large butcher paper or newsprint
bulletin board trim, taped to edge of table to make fence
tempera paints
spoons or brushes for paint
shallow dish of water to clean car
paper towels

ART EXPERIMENT:
1. Cover a table with newsprint or butcher paper.
2. Line the edges of the table with bulletin board trim to form a fence that will keep the car on the table.
3. Spoon some paint anywhere on the paper.
4. Place a toy car on the paper and turn it on.
5. Let the car run through the paint making tracks as it goes.
6. Help the car go through paint and make designs.
7. Turn the car off and remove the battery.
8. Gently rinse wheels and car in a shallow dish of water and dry with paper towels.
9. Replace battery and add more designs to this painting or begin a new one.

VARIATIONS:
- Use an inexpensive remote control car.
- Use any rolling toys and drive or maneuver them by hand through the paint to make designs. (It's a good idea to use only toys that will be used for painting as cleaning them is sometimes difficult.)

A battery uses a chemical reaction to create ELECTRICITY, a flow of charged particles which is one of the most versatile forms of ENERGY. Because of the exchange of electricity through the toy car's motor, energy is transferred and used to move the car through the paint, creating a design.

MOON SCAPE

MATERIALS:
very soft modeling clay or plasticine
flat metal tray
round objects such as –
    ball bearing, marble, tennis ball, orange
tempera paints
paintbrushes
sheet of large drawing paper

ART EXPERIMENT:
1. Spread the soft modeling clay or plasticine over a flat metal tray.
2. Drop a ball-bearing or marble into the clay from different heights. Try 1 ft. (30 cm), 2 ft. (60 cm), and so on.
3. Try different weights of objects from different heights and see what types of designs can be made.
4. Work until a desired relief design is reached. The clay will begin to look a little like the surface of the moon.
5. Add other bits of clay for raised shapes to offset the holes made by dropping objects.
6. Paint the clay surface with a thin coat of tempera paint using one or many colors.
7. Gently lay a piece of large drawing paper over the painted clay.
8. Press and rub the paper's surface with the palm of the hand.
9. Peel off the paper to see the transferred moon scape print.

Note: Clay can be rinsed under the faucet until clean, patted dry with a towel, and used again.

When a ball or marble is dropped on the clay, the force of GRAVITY is pulling the object downward toward the center of the earth. Dropping an object in clay creates holes that look like the craters on the moon. CRATERS are giant holes formed when a meteorite smashes into the moon. Craters are round and have a rim around the edge made by material that is thrown out by the impact.

BALLOON DECORATION

STATIC ELECTRICITY

MATERIALS:

balloons blown up and tied
small torn pieces of paper
confetti

tiny bits of pretty items such as –
   glitter, lace, sequins, sugar, salt
tray or baking pan

ART EXPERIMENT:

1. Sprinkle pretty items into the tray, such as bits of torn paper, confetti, sugar, and sequins to decorate the balloons.
2. Rub a balloon against clothes or hair. (Hint: wool works very well.)
3. Hold the balloon just above the decorations in the tray. (This is the best part!)
4. For a more heavily decorated balloon, roll the balloon directly in decorations or sprinkle them on the balloon.
5. Now decorate another balloon.
6. Continue decorating balloons in this way until the project is complete.

VARIATIONS:

- Use several static electricity balloon decorations as a centerpiece for a kids' party table. The little bits of pretty items will stick to the balloon for a long time.
- Make the balloons fit a special holiday or theme, such as:
  – silver and black balloons with gold and silver bits for an outer space theme
  – red and green balloons with gold sequins and ribbon bits for winter holidays
  – pastel balloons with chopped Easter grass and dyed eggshell bits for spring
  – light blue and white balloons with sugar crystals and silver sequins for ice and snow

STATIC ELECTRICITY is caused by an electrical charge formed in certain materials. When a balloon is rubbed on clothing or hair, it becomes charged with electricity and attracts or pulls the little pieces of paper or granules of sugar towards its surface. The paper and sugar "jump up" off the tray and stick to the electrically charged balloon.

DANCING RABBITS

MATERIALS:
2 thick books
paper
scissors
sheet of Plexiglas
scrap of flannel or silk
table

ART EXPERIMENT:
1. Place two thick books several inches apart on a table.
2. Rest a sheet of Plexiglas from one book to the other.
3. Draw, color, and cut out several small pieces of paper in rabbit shapes or any other shapes.
4. Place them under the Plexiglas.
5. Rub the top of the Plexiglas with the fabric scrap.
6. Watch the paper rabbits dance!

VARIATION:
• Add other materials under the Plexiglas, such as chopped Easter grass, confetti, glitter, and pieces of art tissue.

> *STATIC ELECTRICITY is made when particles in the Plexiglas become charged by rubbing the Plexiglas with silk or flannel. The Plexiglas becomes positively charged and the paper bits become negatively charged. Since opposites attract, the negative paper bits are pulled toward the positive Plexiglas because the paper is attracted to the charge in the Plexiglas. The paper bits "jump up" and stick to the Plexiglas.*

MAGNET PAINTING

MAGNETISM

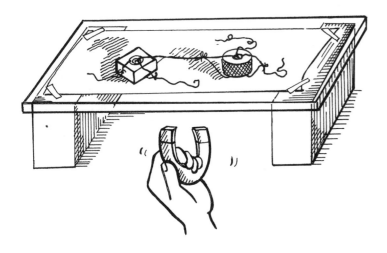

>
> *MAGNETISM is a property of some metals such as iron. Many objects around the house like washers, nuts, bolts, and screws are partly made of iron and will be attracted to a magnet. The force from the magnet can be felt right through many materials, like Plexiglas. When the magnet is moved under the Plexiglas, objects with iron in them will be moved around above the Plexiglas.*

MATERIALS:

blocks
piece of Plexiglas (11" x 14" or
    28 cm x 36 cm or larger)
strong magnet
metal objects such as
    washers, nuts, bolts

embroidery floss (or thread)
tempera paint
paper
tape

ART EXPERIMENT:

1. Place Plexiglas across two large blocks with enough room under the plexiglass to move hands.
2. Tape the paper on top of the Plexiglas.
3. Tie varying lengths of embroidery floss to washers and nuts.
4. Dip the washers or other metal objects in paint and lay them on the paper.
5. Hold a magnet against the underside of the Plexiglas and begin moving the magnet.
6. The magnet will "paint" with the metal objects and embroidery floss as they move over the paper.
7. Remove the objects, dip again in more paint, and continue painting until design is complete.

VARIATIONS:

- Spoon blobs of paint on the paper and drag the objects through the paint with the magnet.
- Experiment with food coloring or watercolors instead of tempera paint.
- Insert a marker through a nut. Place the nut and marker on top of the washer so that marker tip is exposed. Tape the marker, nut, and washer together. Move the magnet underneath the Plexiglas to begin drawing with the marker in the nut (see illustration).

FUNNY FACES

MATERIALS:
drawing paper
colored markers
magnet
box lid
tape
paper clips

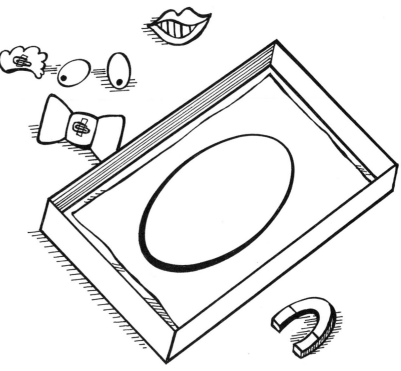

ART EXPERIMENT:
1. Draw and color an oval to represent a face shape in the box lid.
2. On the paper, draw and color facial features including eyes, hair, mouth and nose. Cut these out.
3. Tape paper clips on the backs of each of the facial features.
4. Put all the facial features in the box, paper clip side down.
5. Hold a magnet under the box lid and move the features into place to make a complete face.

VARIATIONS:
- Add additional facial features such as ears, hat, mustache, crown, ribbons, glasses, and others.
- Create other characters in box lids such as a clown, monster, astronaut, or performer.
- Draw other ideas with features to match such as a bowl with fruit, a bank with money, or a garden with flowers.

> *MAGNETISM is a force that causes certain materials to be drawn together or pushed apart. Common objects that contain iron, like paper clips, are attracted to a magnet. By attaching cut-out shapes to a paper clip, the shapes can be moved around with a magnet through the box lid because the magnetic force is strong enough to work through thin cardboard.*

METALLIC DESIGN

MAGNETISM

MATERIALS:
fine steel wool
magnet
heavy paper or light cardboard
old scissors
clear, plastic fixative spray

◆ adult help

ART EXPERIMENT:
1. An adult can cut the steel wool into tiny pieces with the old scissors.
2. Place the magnet on the table. Place a sheet of heavy paper over the magnet.
3. Sprinkle lots of steel wool pieces on the paper and watch them move into a pattern.
4. Move the paper over the magnet until a desired pattern is achieved. Or, move the magnet around to achieve different patterns.
5. Next, spray the pattern of filings with a clear, plastic fixative with the magnet still in place. Let the steel wool design dry on the paper. Then lift the paper and filings off of the magnet.

VARIATIONS:
- Use two bar magnets to make patterns as the poles attract or repel each other.
- Add other metal objects under the paper with the magnets. These pieces may become magnetized and make the patterns more dramatic.
- When the metal painting is dry, add other watercolor designs or glue other collage items to the work.

MAGNETISM is a property of some metals such as the iron in steel wool. The pattern formed by the bits of iron cut from steel wool shows the lines of force around the magnet. A piece of paper will not block the magnetic force and the filings line up along the lines of force making patterns.

MAGNETIC STAGE PLAY

MATERIALS:

construction paper
colored markers
paper clips
scissors
glue
magnets
shoe box

ART EXPERIMENT:

1. Use the construction paper to draw and cut out several characters for a play.
2. Tape or glue tabs made from construction paper on the base of each character.
3. Tape or glue paper clips to the bottom of each tab. The characters are now ready for the play.
4. Turn the shoe box on its side for a stage.
5. Place the characters on the top side of the box.
6. Use another magnet inside the box to move the characters back and forth on the box stage. The magnet will attract or hold to the paper clip through the shoe box and move the characters without touching them.
7. Make up a story and have the paper characters act it out.

VARIATIONS:

- Act out a favorite story or fairy tale with magnetic characters.
- Perform a musical show to a tape recording.

> *MAGNETISM is a force that causes certain materials to be drawn together or pushed apart. The force of magnetism can even travel through thin cardboard. Common objects that contain iron, like paper clips, are attracted to a magnet. By attaching cut-out figures to a paper clip, the attraction of the magnet to the paper clip moves the figures around through the cardboard shoe box.*

MAGNETIC RUBBING

MAGNETISM

MATERIALS:
iron filings
large white paper
bar magnets
other magnets, optional
peeled crayons

ART EXPERIMENT:
1. Lay a bar magnet under a heavy sheet of white paper.
2. Sprinkle iron filings over the paper.
3. Place a second sheet of white paper over the filings which have formed a design due to the pull of the magnet on the filings.
4. Rub the peeled crayon on its side back and forth over the paper, capturing the design of the iron filings.
5. Remove the filings and the magnet.

VARIATIONS:
• Lay two magnets with like poles almost together (that is, with the two N's or the two S's almost together) and make a crayon rubbing of this magnetic design.
• Place the bar magnets with opposite poles together (that is, with the N from one almost touching the S from the other). Make a crayon rubbing of this design.
• Pour iron filings on a blank piece of paper. Move the magnet under the paper trying to form different designs with the filings.

> *MAGNETISM is a property of some metals such as the iron filings. The pattern formed by the iron filings shows the lines of force from the magnet. A magnet has ends, called poles. One end, the north pole, is ATTRACTED to the other end, the south pole. The lines of magnetic force can be seen between the poles of the magnet when iron filings are sprinkled on white paper with the magnet underneath. When like poles of bar magnets are placed together they REPEL, or push away from each other. ATTRACTING and REPELLING magnets show patterns with the iron filings whose designs can be captured by a crayon rubbing.*

REACTIONS AND CHANGE
chapter 4

CANDLE COLORING

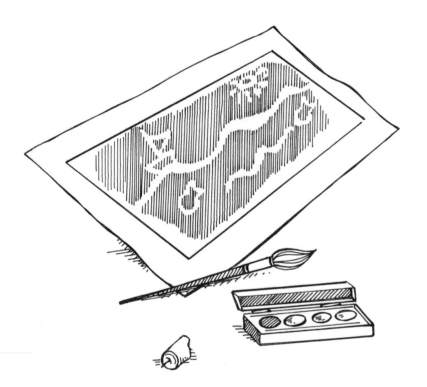

MATERIALS:
old candles
white drawing paper
watercolors
paintbrush
newspaper

ART EXPERIMENT:
1. Cover the table with newspaper.
2. Draw with the candle on white paper, pressing firmly.
3. Next, paint over the candle markings with watercolor paints.

VARIATIONS:
- Draw with crayon and paint over this with black or dark purple tempera paint thinned with water.
- Use bright colors and press hard with crayon until the sheet of paper is entirely covered with crayon. Then paint over this with thick black paint. Dry. Scratch a design through the black paint with scissors or a paper clip.

The watercolors will ADHERE or soak into the paper, but not where it is covered with candle wax. The watercolors are attracted to the paper by a force called ADHESION. But the watercolors stay separate from the candle wax drawing by a stronger force called COHESION. (See page 95, White Resist.)

94   reactions and change

WHITE RESIST

MATERIALS:

white crayon
thin tempera paint in cups
paintbrushes
white paper
newspaper to cover table

ART EXPERIMENT:

1. Draw a picture with white crayon on white paper.
2. Paint over the drawing with thinned tempera paint. Dry.

VARIATIONS:

- Draw with many colors of crayons for a crayon resist.
- Experiment with black paint as compared to yellow paint.

> The thin tempera paint will ADHERE or soak into the paper, but not where it is covered with wax from the white crayon. The thin tempera paint molecules are attracted to the paper by a force called ADHESION. But the paint stays separate from the waxed paper by a stronger force called COHESION. (See page 94, Candle Coloring.)

IMMISCIBLES

IMMISCIBLE

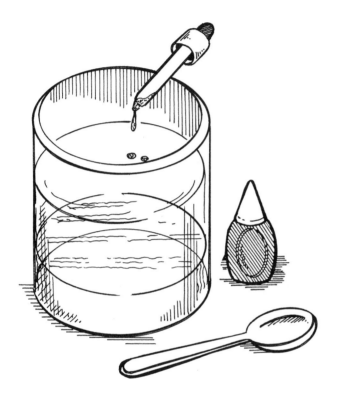

MATERIALS:
water
cooking oil
food coloring
clear glass jar
eyedropper
spoon

ART EXPERIMENT:
1. Pour a little water into the jar.
2. Pour cooking oil on top of the water and watch them separate into layers.
3. Try stirring them together. Then let stand.
5. Using the eyedropper, carefully drop one or two drops of food color into the oil. The color will sit in tiny balls because food color is immiscible with oil.
6. Push the color balls into the water with a spoon.
7. Watch them burst into a cloud of color.

VARIATIONS:
- Experiment with kitchen utensils to break up the color balls, such as an eggbeater, wire whisk, or fork.
- Use a watercolor paintbrush dipped into the color balls and see if it is possible to paint with them on paper.

Oil and water are IMMISCIBLE which means they will not mix. Oil and water stay separate even when shaken, stirred, or blended. The food coloring consists of mostly water and therefore will not mix with the oil. As soon as the food coloring is pushed through the oil and touches the water, it DIFFUSES throughout the water in a burst of color. Food coloring and water are MISCIBLE which means they can mix.

CHROMATOGRAPHY

MATERIALS:
dowel rod
2 stacks of blocks
masking tape
inks or food coloring
jars
paper clips
absorbent paper
eyedropper

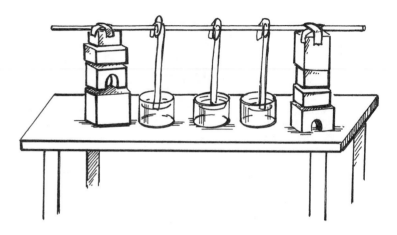

ART EXPERIMENT:
1. Suspend the dowel between two stacks of blocks over a table. Tape to hold.
2. Mix two or more of the inks or food colors into separate jars.
3. Use paper clips to clip strips of absorbent paper to the dowel, one strip for each jar.
4. Drop a small drop of color on the end of each strip.
5. Hang strips with ends just touching the water in the jars. Colors will travel up the strip and separate into colored bands.

VARIATIONS:
- Drop a dot of color in the middle of a coffee filter and watch the colors separate. Dry.
- Moisten a paper towel. Drop a dot of color on the wet towel and watch the colors separate. Dry.
- Separate watercolor paints, felt pens, and tempera paints.
- Use the colored strips for weaving, chains, or other art ideas.

The process of separating colors or PIGMENTS is called CHROMATOGRAPHY. The paper strips absorb colored water from the jars and the colors are carried up the absorbent paper strip, dissolving as they absorb. The different colored pigments in each jar travel at different speeds and will separate into different bands of color. The pigments that dissolve quickly move up the paper the farthest and fastest. Pigments that dissolve slowly travel only a short distance and take the longest. Some of the inks and food coloring contain many pigments and will have many bands of color separating on the paper strip. Other inks and food coloring contain only one pigment and will have only one band of separated color on the paper strip.

ERUPTING COLORS

SOLUBILITY / EMULSION

MATERIALS:
cake pan with edges
milk
food coloring
liquid dishwashing detergent

ART EXPERIMENT:
1. Pour milk into the cake pan until the bottom is covered.
2. Sprinkle several drops of food coloring on the milk.
3. Add a few drops of dishwashing detergent in the centers of the largest drops of coloring.
4. Watch the resulting eruption of colors.
5. If erupting slows down, try adding more food coloring and then more detergent. If the experiment will not work after awhile, begin again from clean milk and new drops of color and detergent.
6. When experiment is complete, pan washes easily in warm water.

VARIATIONS:
* Make smaller experiments in custard cups and try different combinations of colors to see what new colors can be created.
* Use a clear baking pan. Have someone hold the experiment above eye level and watch the erupting colors from the bottom of the pan.

Milk contains water and fat. These two substances do not mix. Even though the milk looks like one substance, it is really separate water and fat. Detergent is a substance that will mix with water or fat. When detergent is dropped into milk, one end of the detergent molecule attaches to fat in the milk and the other end of the detergent molecule attaches to the water which causes a boiling effect.

THE VOLCANO

PRESSURE / GASES

MATERIALS:
soda bottle
baking pan
moist soil
1 T. (15 ml) baking soda
1 cup (250 ml) vinegar
red food coloring
outdoors

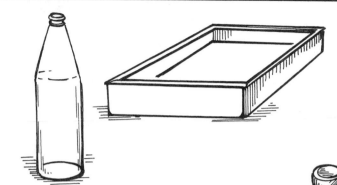

ART EXPERIMENT:
1. Place the baking pan on the grass, and set the soda bottle in the center of the pan.
2. Mound and shape the moist soil around the bottle to form a mountain. Bring the soil right up to the top of the bottle's opening but do not get soil inside the bottle.
3. Pour 1 T. (15 ml) baking soda into the bottle.
4. Color 1 cup (250 ml) vinegar with the red food coloring.
5. Pour the colored vinegar into the bottle. Stand back and watch red foam spray out the top and down the mountain of dirt like lava from a volcano.

Baking soda reacts with vinegar to produce CARBON DIOXIDE GAS which builds up enough PRESSURE to force the foaming liquid out of the top of the bottle.

reactions and change 99

CRYSTAL DESIGN

CRYSTALS

MATERIALS:
pipe cleaner
clear cup
1/2 cup (125 ml) hot water
1/3 cup (80 ml) salt
spoon
pencil
string

◆ adult help

PROCEDURE:
1. Bend a pipe cleaner in any shape.
2. Pour 1/2 cup (125 ml) of very hot water into the clear cup.
3. Add about 1/3 cup (80 ml) salt to the water a spoonful at a time. Stir and dissolve after each spoonful. Add salt until no more will dissolve.
4. Curl one end of the pipe cleaner around the middle of a pencil.
5. Place the pencil across the top of the cup. Be sure the pipe cleaner hangs deep into the hot, salty water.
6. Move this hot, crystal growing cup into a place where it will not be disturbed and where it can be watched closely.
7. After a few hours, signs of crusty crystals will appear on the pipe cleaner.
8. Watch the crystals change each day. When most of the liquid is gone from the cup, remove the pipe cleaner from the cup and slide it off the pencil.
9. Carefully tie a string onto the top of the crystal shape and hang it where it can be seen and enjoyed.

Before salt is ground into the grains commonly used in food, salt is a large chunk and is a CRYSTAL. However, salt is usually seen when it is ground into small CRYSTALS. When the salt crystals are dissolved in the hot water, the molecules of salt spread throughout the water. Then, as the water EVAPORATES, the salt molecules lineup in a regular pattern to form a crystal again. Sometimes, if the conditions are just right, a really big, block-shaped crystal will form.

VARIATIONS:
• Add food coloring to the water in step 2.
• Hang the pipecleaners from a string as a decoration.

CRYSTAL PAINT

MATERIALS:
freezing night or freezer
water
watercolor paint and brushes
plastic wrap
cookie sheet
white drawing paper

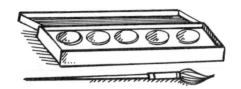

ART EXPERIMENT:
1. Paint clear water on the white drawing paper.
2. Then paint the wet paper with watercolor paint, letting colors run together.
3. Immediately cover the wet painting with a sheet of plastic wrap. Place on a cookie sheet.
4. Leave the painting outside all night to freeze, or place in the freezer.
5. Next day, pull the plastic wrap off the frozen painting and observe the crystal creation.

VARIATION:
- Cover the painting with a second sheet of wet paper. Smooth with the hands. Freeze. Thaw slightly. Peel the papers apart for two frozen paintings.

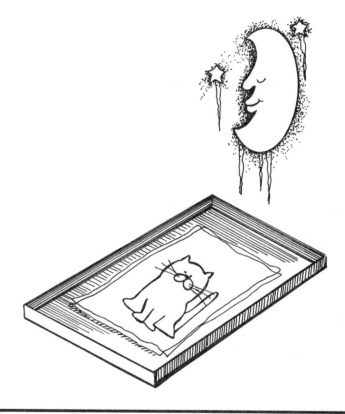

First the watercolor paints DIFFUSE into the clear water on the paper which causes the colors to run together. When the paper is placed in the freezer, the molecules of colored water slow down until they change from liquid to solid. This begins to occur at the FREEZING point of water which is 32 °F (0 °C). When the molecules of colored water line up in a regular pattern, the colored water forms ice CRYSTALS.

CRYSTAL BUBBLES

FREEZING / CRYSTALS

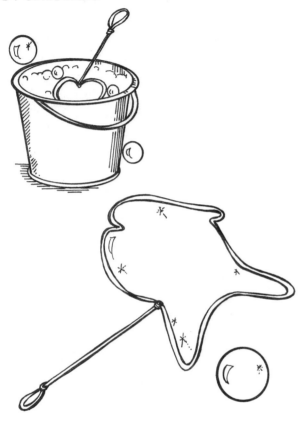

Extra Strong Bubble Recipe:

Mix together -

    3-4 T. (45-60 ml) of soap flakes or soap powder (Fels or Ivory)

    4 cups (1 l) hot water

    Let stand for several days.

    Stir in a large spoonful of sugar.

The bubble mixture is ready to use.

To make bubble blowers:

    Save a piece of wire.

    Bend the wire into any shape. Be sure to "close" the shape.

ART EXPERIMENT:

1. Go outside on a very cold day (32°F or 0°C or colder) when there is no wind.
2. Dip a bubble blower into the soap mixture and gently blow a large bubble. Try not to let the bubble blow away.
3. The bubble should begin to freeze with tiny crystals forming over the surface.
4. The bubble will freeze completely into an ice crystal ball.

VARIATIONS:

- Colored wire from scrap telephone cables works very well and is free from telephone installers.
- Use a slotted spoon as a bubble blower.
- Use a clean fly swatter as a bubble blower.
- Experiment with other items for blowing bubbles.

At normal room temperature bubble soap is a LIQUID, but if you cool it enough or freeze it, it will become a SOLID. In the right conditions CRYSTALS will form when a bubble freezes and the molecules in the bubble arrange themselves in a pattern. If the bubble is cooled slowly, the molecules have time to line up just right and form CRYSTALS.

CRYSTAL NEEDLES

MATERIALS:
black paper
scissors
lid from a large jar
1 cup (250 ml) water
4 T. (60 ml) Epsom salts

ART EXPERIMENT:
1. Cut a circle of black paper that will fit inside the jar lid.
2. Place the circle in the lid.
3. Fill the measuring cup with 1 cup (250 ml) water.
4. Add 4 T. (60 ml) of Epsom salts to the water and stir.
5. Pour the salty water in the lid.
6. Let the mixture in the lid stand for one day. Observe the needle-shaped crystals on the black paper.

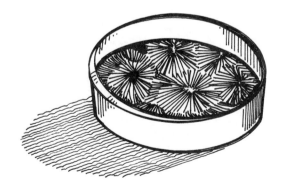

 Epsom salts molecules line up in an orderly pattern and form needle-shaped CRYSTALS *as the water slowly evaporates from the solution. The salt molecules stack together just like building blocks. The needle shape of the crystal is determined by the shape of the salt molecule. This is why table salt and Epsom salts do not have the same crystal shapes.*

8 & up | CAUTION

CRYSTAL INK

CRYSTALS / EVAPORATION

MATERIALS:
3 t. (15 ml) salt
1/4 cup (60 ml) water
warm oven (150°F or 75°C)
paintbrush
1 sheet black construction paper

◆ Adult help with oven.

ART EXPERIMENT:
1. Add 3 t. (15 ml) salt to 1/4 cup (60 ml) water.
2. Paint a design or message on the black paper with the salt solution. Stir the salt with the brush each time the brush is used to paint.
3. Turn off the oven and place the paper in the oven on top of the wire racks. Heat for 5 minutes or until the design dries.
4. Remove the dry design from the oven. The design or message will appear as white, shiny crystals.

When water EVAPORATES, the liquid water changes into a gas or water vapor and enters the air. Dry salt CRYSTALS are left on the paper because the salt does not evaporate. Heating the paper in the warm oven speeds up the evaporation process. Black paper makes the white crystals easier to see.

PLASTIC MILK

CASEIN

MATERIALS:

10 oz. (.3 l) milk
saucepan, stove
spoon
1 T. (15 ml) vinegar
old muslin sheet

jar
rubber band
cookie cutter, optional
tempera paint

◆ adult help

ART EXPERIMENT:
1. Warm 10 oz. (.3 l) of milk in a pan over low heat but do not boil. Adult help suggested.
2. Add 1 T. (15 ml) vinegar and stir until a white rubbery material forms in the milk. This is called casein.
3. Stretch a square of muslin over the opening of the jar and hold in place with a rubber band around the neck of the jar.
4. Squeeze the milk through the muslin into the jar until the rubbery casein is left.
5. Push the casein into a mold such as a cookie cutter or shape it by hand into any shape.
6. Let it set for a few days so the casein dries and hardens.
7. Decorate the plastic milk with paint.

VARIATIONS:
- To make a casein pin, push a safety pin into the back of the mold while casein is still soft. Then harden and decorate.
- To make a casein necklace or pendant, push a loop of wire or a paper clip into the back of the mold while casein is still soft. Then harden and decorate. String a piece of yarn or cord through the wire or paper clip to wear as a necklace.

Milk contains a protein called CASEIN. Cheese, made from milk, is mostly casein. Casein is also used to make plastic, glue, and paint. Cooking milk with vinegar causes the casein to separate from the other substances in milk and become a moldable substance similar in characteristics to PLASTIC.

MARSHMALLOW TOWER

ENGINEERING

MATERIALS:
package of toothpicks
miniature marshmallows, stale

ART EXPERIMENT:
1. Stick a toothpick into a stale marshmallow.
2. Add another marshmallow to the other end of the toothpick.
3. Now add another toothpick, another marshmallow, and so on.
4. Keep adding and building until a tower can stand alone.

VARIATIONS:
- Use modeling clay balls and toothpicks instead of marshmallows.
- Build a bridge between two chairs placed 1 ft. (100 cm) apart.
- Build a tall structure.
- Build a long structure.
- Use toothpicks with glue instead of marshmallows for a more permanent structure.
- Use only 10 marshmallows with 15 toothpicks, and then try using 15 marshmallows and 10 toothpicks. Which one is stronger?
- Make the same type of structures using straws and masking tape or rolls of newspaper and masking tape.
- Dye white miniature marshmallows in food coloring and water. Dry.
- Use fruit colored miniature marshmallows.

Many bridges and towers are made with triangular shapes. A wide base and narrow top make a sturdy structure. Gravity is always "pulling things down" towards the earth. When ENGINEERS *build structures, they are discovering how to keep the structures up.*

BUILDING BEANS

MATERIALS:
large dried beans
bowl of water
strainer
wooden toothpicks

ART EXPERIMENT:
1. Soak the beans overnight in the bowl of water.
2. Strain the water off the beans.
3. Stick a toothpick in one bean.
4. Continue sticking beans and toothpicks together to make a structure.
5. When finished, let the bean structure dry overnight.

VARIATIONS:
- Build a structure with marshmallows and toothpicks.
- Build a structure with balls of clay and toothpicks.
- Build a structure with soaked dry peas and toothpicks. Dry.
- Build a structure with fresh peas from the pod and toothpicks. Dry.

 Building with beans is a good way to experiment and learn about strong STRUCTURES. BALANCE *helps make structures strong.* GRAVITY *is always "pulling things down" toward the earth. When engineers build structures, they are discovering how to "keep things up."*

SPAGHETTI PAINTING

DISSOLVE / GLUTEN

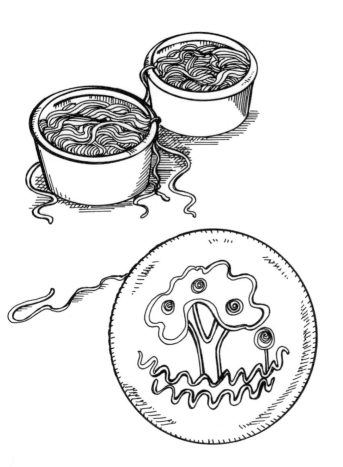

MATERIALS:
cooked, drained spaghetti
4 glass bowls
food coloring
spoons

ART EXPERIMENT:
1. Place small amounts of cooked, drained spaghetti in four small glass bowls.
2. Add drops of food coloring to each bowl, one color for each.
3. Stir until spaghetti is coated and colored with food coloring.
4. Remove a strand of spaghetti from a bowl and arrange on a paper plate in any design.
5. Continue to add more colored spaghetti to the design. Spaghetti will stick without glue.
6. Let the spaghetti picture dry overnight.

VARIATION:
- Cook and color other pastas for "pasta paintings."

Spaghetti is made from flour. Flour on the surface of the spaghetti DISSOLVES in the hot water to form its own glue or paste called GLUTEN. It can be very sticky. As this natural glue dries, it hardens and bonds the spaghetti to the paper.

SANDPAPER DESIGNS

MATERIALS:
sheet of fine sandpaper
pieces of colorful yarn
scissors

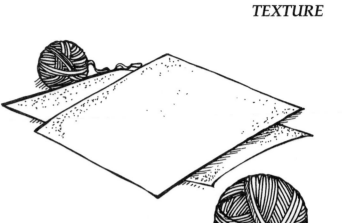

ART EXPERIMENT:
1. Place a sheet of fine sandpaper on the table.
2. Place pieces of colorful yarn on the sandpaper. (Yarn will stick to the sandpaper much like Velcro sticks to itself.)
3. Move yarn pieces to different positions until the design or picture is complete.
4. Take apart and begin again if desired.

VARIATIONS:
- Sandpaper can be made by covering a sheet of heavy paper with glue and then covering the glue with sand. When dry, shake off excess sand.
- Experiment with other items which might stick to the sandpaper, such as lace scraps or embroidery floss.

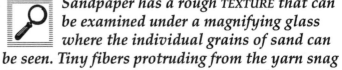
Sandpaper has a rough TEXTURE that can be examined under a magnifying glass where the individual grains of sand can be seen. Tiny fibers protruding from the yarn snag the grains of sand and stick to the sandpaper.

INVISIBLE PAINT

ACID / BASE

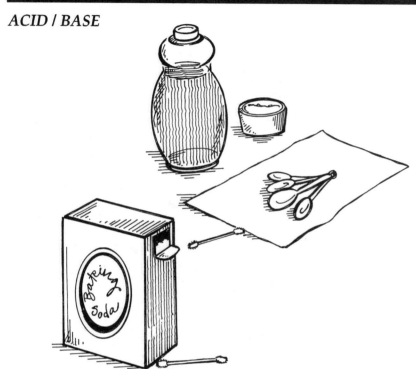

MATERIALS:
cups
4 T. (60 ml) baking soda
4 T. (60 ml) water
cotton swab
sheet of white paper
purple grape juice

ART EXPERIMENT:
1. To make the paint, dissolve 4 T. (60 ml) of baking soda in 4 T. (60 ml) of water in a cup.
2. Dip the cotton swab in the paint mixture and make a picture on the white paper.
3. Let the watery picture dry completely.
4. Next, brush grape juice over the paper to reveal the painting. The picture mysteriously appears in blue-green colors.

Many common foods like vinegar and lemon have a sour taste and are called ACIDS. *Other foods like milk and baking soda are called* BASES. *These foods and many other substances have different chemical makeups that make them either an acid or a base. Grape juice is an* ACID/BASE INDICATOR. *This means that it will determine the acid/base level of a substance by changing color. When grape juice touches the baking soda painting, the painting changes from clear to blue-green indicating that baking soda is a base.*

MAGIC CABBAGE

MATERIALS:

fresh red cabbage
knife
pot
stove
water
strainer
bowl
paintbrush
white paper
vinegar

◆ adult help

ART EXPERIMENT:

1. Cut the cabbage into small pieces with a knife.
2. Fill a pot half full of water and put the cabbage pieces in it.
3. Adult step. Put the pot on the stove and bring to a boil. Boil for about one minute. Then remove it from the heat.
4. Let the pot set for about 20 minutes.
5. Strain the colored cabbage water into a bowl. Set the cabbage aside to eat later.
7. With a paintbrush, use the colored cabbage juice to make a picture on the paper.
8. Let the cabbage juice painting dry completely.
9. Next, brush a little vinegar on the painting to reveal the magic picture. The juice should turn from purple to pink.

Many common foods like vinegar and lemon have a sour taste and are called ACIDS. *Other foods like milk and baking soda are called* BASES. *Cabbage juice is an* ACID/BASE INDICATOR *which means that it will determine the acid/base level of a substance by changing color. When vinegar touches the cabbage juice painting, the purple painting changes to pink indicating that vinegar is an acid.*

GASES

MATERIALS:

1 package yeast
1-1/2 cups (375 ml) warm water
1 t. (5 ml) salt
1 T. (15 ml) sugar
4 cups (1 l) flour
1 egg, beaten
salt (optional)

large bowl
spoon
greased cookie sheet
pastry brush
oven, 350°F (180°C)

◆ adult help

ART EXPERIMENT:

The dough –
1. Measure 1-1/2 cups (375 ml) warm water into the large bowl.
2. Sprinkle yeast into water and stir until soft.
3. Add 1 t. (5 ml) salt, 1 T. (15 ml) sugar, and 4 cups (1 l) flour.
4. Mix and knead the dough with hands. Dough should be smooth and elastic, not sticky.

The sculptures –
1. Roll and twist dough into any shapes such as letters, animals, and unique shapes.
2. Place the dough sculptures on a greased cookie sheet.
3. Let rise until double in size.
4. Brush each sculpture with beaten egg.
5. Sprinkle with salt (optional).
6. Bake for 12 to 15 minutes at 350°F (180°C) until sculptures are firm and golden brown. Cool slightly. Eat and enjoy!

> *Yeast in the pretzel dough makes it puff up, or rise. A chemical reaction between the yeast, the flour, and the sugar causes the production of carbon dioxide* GAS *that causes the dough to rise. The same kind of gas can be made by mixing baking soda and vinegar which causes foaming. (See page 99, The Volcano.)*

NATURE
AND EARTH
chapter 5

BARK RUBBINGS

BARK

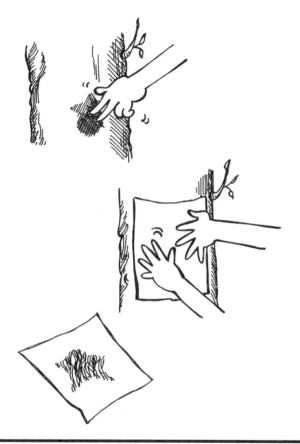

MATERIALS:
finger paint
outdoors
trees
paper
paintbrush
bucket of water
towel
scrub brush

ART EXPERIMENT:
1. Fingerpaint on a small area of tree bark.
2. Clean hands.
3. Press and smooth the paper over the painted bark.
4. Slowly peel the paper off the bark and look at the tree bark print. Dry.
5. Meanwhile, wash and scrub the tree bark with clear water and a scrub brush until no trace of paint remains.

VARIATIONS:
- Make paint rubbings of rocks, leaves, sidewalks, bricks, and other outdoor objects.
- Combine two or three rubbings on one sheet of paper, overlapping textures and paint colors.
- Press imprints of outdoor objects into plasticine or playdough.

The BARK of a TREE must stretch as the tree grows. Some trees have very stretchy bark which looks smooth because it stretches so easily. Other trees have less stretchy bark which cracks when the tree gets big. This is why some trees have rough bark with deep grooves. A Bark Rubbing is a way to see the patterns of stretching and growing of bark that covers and protects trees.

SHOE POLISH LEAVES

MATERIALS:

shoe polish
fresh leaves
white paper
old cloth
brayer or rolling pin
outdoors

ART EXPERIMENT:

1. Rub shoe polish on the back of a fresh leaf with an old cloth.
2. Place the leaf polish side down on white paper.
3. Cover the leaf with another piece of white paper.
4. Roll the brayer or rolling pin firmly over the paper-covered leaf.
5. Remove the paper slowly and peel the leaf off by the stem. A leaf print will remain showing veins, stem, and leaf imprint.

VARIATIONS:

- Use a variety of shoe polish colors and types of leaves.
- Experiment with papers such as tracing paper, waxed paper, textured paper, and colored paper.
- Use ink from an ink pad instead of shoe polish.
- Use paint instead of shoe polish.

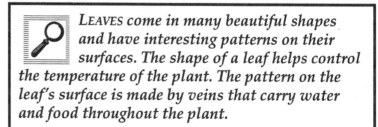

LEAVES come in many beautiful shapes and have interesting patterns on their surfaces. The shape of a leaf helps control the temperature of the plant. The pattern on the leaf's surface is made by veins that carry water and food throughout the plant.

NATURE SPRAY

PLANTS

MATERIALS:
tempera paint in a cup
toothbrush
screen sieve
paper
nature collection –
– pine branches
– leaves
– flowers
table covered with newspaper
outdoors

ART EXPERIMENT:
1. Trace the outside edge of the screen sieve on the paper to make a circle.
2. Collect a variety of small pine branches, leaves, and flowers.
3. Make an arrangement inside the sieve's circle on the paper.
4. Gently place the sieve over the arrangement.
4. Dip the toothbrush in the paint and scrape back and forth on the screen of the sieve making a spray of paint.
5. Continue scraping the toothbrush across the sieve until the paint is heavy enough.
6. Very carefully remove the sieve.
7. Let the nature collection remain in position until the paint is dry, then remove them. Stencils of the branches, leaves, and flowers will be left.

VARIATIONS:
Spray paint over:
– designs cut from paper
– pieces of masking tape stuck to paper and peeled off when paint is dry
– small toys and junk items such as Legos, nuts, bolts, and magnetic letters

> *The* PLANT *blocks paint from reaching the paper. When the plant is removed, there will be a* NEGATIVE PICTURE *of the plant remaining. The shape of the plant remains the same, something like a* SHADOW *or* SILHOUETTE *of the natural plant.*

PLANT IMPRINTS

PIGMENTS

MATERIALS:
fresh leaves
fresh flowers
white fabric
hammer
wooden board
thumbtacks
outdoors

ART EXPERIMENT:
1. Create an arrangement of the leaves and flowers on the wooden board.
2. Tack a piece of white fabric over the arrangement.
3. Next, hammer all over the fabric area crushing the leaves and flowers beneath the fabric.
4. Remove the thumbtacks from the fabric and look at the imprint designs left on the fabric.

VARIATIONS:
- Cover the plants with a sheet of heavy paper and repeat the above hammering process.
- Cover the plants with a sheet of heavy paper and make a plant rubbing with the side of a peeled crayon or stick of charcoal.

The colors seen in fresh leaves and flowers come from chemicals called PIGMENTS. *Crushing the plants with a hammer releases pigments that stain the white fabric. People throughout history have crushed plants and used natural pigments as paint and dye.*

SYMMETRY PRINTS

SYMMETRY

MATERIALS:
2 apples
knife and adult to help cut
cutting board
tempera paint in a dish or styrofoam tray
paper

◆ adult help

ART EXPERIMENT:
1. Use the knife to cut one apple in half top to bottom. Then cut another apple in half across the middle.
2. Choose one half from each apple to use for printing with paint, and the other halves to eat.
3. Press the first apple half into paint and then press on paper. Look at the symmetry, which means that the two sides match and are exactly the same in design.
4. Next, press the other apple half into paint and then on to the paper for a different symmetry design.
5. Continue making apple prints in any design desired.

VARIATIONS:
- Using the apple half cut top to bottom, cut that half in half again, which is a quarter of an apple. The two apple quarters are symmetrical too. Use for prints.
- Try cutting oranges, bananas, peaches, or pears. Use some symmetrical parts for printing, and some parts for eating.

The apple cut top to bottom shows BILATERAL SYMMETRY. *This means that if a line were drawn through the middle of the apple half, the designs and shape of the two sides would match. The apple cut through the middle shows* RADIAL SYMMETRY. *This means that all the designs radiating from the center part of the apple are the same pattern.*

STICKY PICTURES

MATERIALS:
petroleum jelly
paper plates
dandelion seeds
very fine grass clippings
sink, soap, towel
table covered with newspaper
outdoors

ART EXPERIMENT:
1. Smear petroleum jelly on a paper plate with fingers. Set the plate on newspaper on a table.
2. Wash and dry hands thoroughly.
3. Hold the seeds and grass clippings above the paper plate in the hands.
4. Blow the seeds out of the hands so that they land on the paper plate and stick.

VARIATIONS:
- Smear petroleum jelly on a paper plate and hang it outside. Check on it later to see what has stuck to it.
- Smear glue on a paper plate and hang it outside to catch airborne bits of things to see what surprises are in the air.

> *Petroleum jelly is a thick, greasy substance. Small, lightweight materials will stick to a plate covered with petroleum jelly. Studying the airborne materials which land in the sticky jelly is a good way to learn about the AIR we breathe. Some things carried by the air are seeds, spores, pollen, and dust.*

STENCIL LEAVES

LEAVES

MATERIALS:
fresh leaves
rubber cement
tempera paint in cups
paintbrushes
paper
outdoors

ART EXPERIMENT:
1. Glue leaves to the paper using rubber cement.
2. Dry well for 1/2 hour or more.
3. Use the tempera paint and paintbrushes to paint over the leaves and paper. (Paint gently over the edges of the leaves so leaves do not peel off.)
4. Let the painting dry completely (overnight is good).
5. Peel the leaves off of the paper carefully and a natural stencil design will be left on the paper.

VARIATIONS:
- Trace leaf shapes on old file folders and cut out. Use both shapes for stencils – the leaf and the hole from the cut out leaf.
- Add a sprinkle of salt to the paint for an interesting effect.
- Do this art experiment with other shapes or flat objects instead of leaves.
- Spatter paint from a toothbrush or shake it from a paint brush across the leaves. Cover work area with newspaper and artist with an apron before beginning. Works well to place paper inside a box with sides to catch spatters.

Leaves come in many beautiful SHAPES and have interesting PATTERNS on their surfaces. The shape of a leaf helps control the temperature of the plant. The pattern on the leaf's surface is made by veins that carry water and food throughout the plant. Creating Stencil Leaves shows the relationship between beauty and function in nature.

TREE ARTS

MATERIALS:
paints
paintbrushes
crayons
pencils
paper
outdoor area with trees

ART EXPERIMENT:
The following five ideas are ways to look at trees more closely while creating beautiful art –
1. With the paints and brushes, paint a picture of a tree using just twelve brush strokes.
2. With black paint, paint a silhouette of a tree.
3. Color an entire piece of paper with black crayon. Color hard and bright. Next, scratch a picture of trees in the crayon with a straightened out paper clip. This is called an etching.
4. Draw or paint leaves while looking at them closely.
5. Take paper and crayon outside and make rubbings of different tree barks.

VARIATIONS:
* Save all five art experiments in a booklet stapled together.
* Think of other ways to paint, draw, sculpt, sew, or design tree art.

> *Scientists and artists both must develop the skill of* OBSERVATION *or looking closely at things and noting their details. Art and science combine in Tree Arts as the details and characteristics of trees are studied and art is created.*

INDOOR BIRD TRACKS

ANIMAL TRACKS / FOSSILS

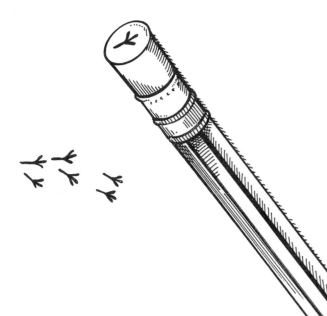

MATERIALS:
pencil with eraser
ballpoint pen
note cards or paper

ART EXPERIMENT:
1. Use the ballpoint pen to draw a small bird track on the eraser of an ordinary pencil.
2. Press the eraser down on the note card or paper.
3. Make easy track patterns.
4. When the tracks become hard to see, draw more ink on the eraser with the pen and make more tracks.

VARIATIONS:
- Design other tiny animal tracks such as mice, gerbils, ants, imaginary creatures, or tiny human feet.
- Make real tracks on large butcher paper by walking in paint and then walking on the paper. Use pretty colors and different kinds of shoes, boots, bare feet, and even skates. Have a tub of water handy for clean up.
- Find animal tracks in the snow, mud, or sand. Copy the tracks on a pencil eraser and recreate the same animal track pattern as it appears in the snow, mud, or sand.

> *Much can be learned from observing* ANIMAL TRACKS. *Sometimes the tracks can tell a story. Scientists who study animal tracks can tell what kind of animal made the tracks, how big it was, and what it was doing when the tracks were made. Sometimes* FOSSIL *animal tracks can be found in very old rock that was once mud. Scientists have learned a great deal about extinct animals like the dinosaurs from these fossil tracks.*

GRASS PATTERNS

MATERIALS:
cardboard
scissors
patch of grass
sunlight
rocks
outdoors

CHLOROPHYLL

ART EXPERIMENT:
1. Ask for adult permission before beginning this activity.
2. Cut cardboard shapes from left-over cardboard boxes.
3. Arrange the cardboard shapes on a patch of green grass.
4. Place a rock or brick on each shape to hold it in place.
5. Leave the shapes in place for several days.
6. Then lift the shapes and examine the grass underneath. Notice that the grass looks yellow.
7. The grass will recover slowly and completely as the sun and rain reach the yellow grass. Water the yellowed areas with a hose or sprinkler to speed recovery.

VARIATIONS:
*   Cut letters out of cardboard and spell out words, names, or messages.
*   Design a celebration or holiday theme pattern in the grass.

The green color in plants comes from a substance called CHLOROPHYLL *which helps the plant use sunshine to make energy, much like animals use food to make energy. When the sunlight is blocked, the chlorophyll is reduced and the green color of the grass fades. The grass turns yellow because it cannot survive without light and starts to die. But when sunlight again reaches the grass, the green will return, especially if the grass is also watered.*

SAND DRAWINGS

WEATHERING

MATERIALS:
two rocks (sandstone works very well)
dark paper (blue, purple, black, green)
white glue
magnifying glass

ART EXPERIMENT:
1. Draw any design on the paper with white glue.
2. Hold two rocks, one in each hand, and rub them together over the paper and glue design. Sand is formed by the rubbing action and will stick in the glue to make a sand drawing.
3. Let sand drawing dry overnight.

VARIATIONS:
- Grind sand from the rocks into a box until a 1/4 cup (60 ml) or so has been ground. Use a magnifying glass to look at the shapes of the grains of sand. Use this sand to sprinkle on glue to make a sand drawing.
- Pound rocks into powder on a sidewalk or larger rock with a hammer. Wear eye protection. Use the powdered sand to make Sand Drawings.

> *Sand is made of a variety of crushed and ground materials such as rocks, shells, bones, and plants. The rubbing and bumping together of rocks as wind and water grind them is called* WEATHERING. *Weathered rock will someday become soil, sand, or be reformed into new rocks.*

SAND GARDEN

SAND / ROCKS

MATERIALS:
sandbox
items from nature such as –
    rocks
    burrs
    twigs
plastic cups, containers, boxes
water
outdoors

ART EXPERIMENT:
1. Moisten the sand in the sandbox with water. Stir with hands until sand holds a shape.
2. Pack sand into a container. Then turn it over in the sandbox so the shape comes out in one piece.
3. Add more shapes of sand from packed containers to the sandbox.
4. Decorate the shapes with twigs, rocks, pebbles, burrs, or other items from nature.
5. When complete, save the project or return sandbox to original condition.

VARIATIONS:
- Create a desert scene using burrs for tumbleweeds and twigs for cactus.
- Create a variety of environments using materials and collections of toys, nature items, etc. such as:
  - – mountain
  - – seaside
  - – park

One way sand is made is by crushing or grinding rock into tiny grains that are many different sizes. Some sand grains are so small that they are powdery in TEXTURE which can be examined under a magnifying glass. When mixed with water, some of the finest grains of sand make a mud that helps the sand hold together. Sometimes there is a chemical in sand that acts like a glue when mixed with water to help hold the sand grains together. In nature, when sand and water press down very hard for a long time, new rock will be made. One type of rock formed this way is called SANDSTONE.

DRIED SEAWEED PRINT

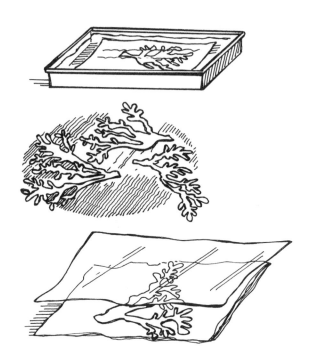

MATERIALS:

fresh seaweed
shallow pan filled with water
heavy paper

waxed paper or plastic film
old newspaper
permanent marking pen

◆ adult help

ART EXPERIMENT:
1. Sink the heavy paper to the bottom of the shallow pan filled with water.
2. Float a piece of seaweed on top of the paper.
3. Carefully lift out the paper while allowing the water to run off, but keeping the seaweed on the paper.
4. Place the wet paper and seaweed on several thicknesses of newspaper to dry.
5. Cover the paper and seaweed with waxed paper or thin plastic film.
6. Use the permanent pen to write a statement about the seaweed or add additional designs on the plastic film or waxed paper, if desired.
7. Repeat this procedure with other seaweeds, placing each piece of paper and seaweed on top of the first in a stack.
8. When all the seaweeds are stacked, cover with a thick layer of newspaper to absorb excess water.
9. Finally, put the whole stack of papers and seaweeds in a flat place with some weight on top (under a rug is very good).
10. Change the newspapers daily until the seaweed is dry.
11. Peel the waxed paper or plastic film off of the paper and a pressed and dried seaweed display will remain pressed to the waxed paper or plastic film.
12. Display seaweed print in a window or keep a collection of prints in a notebook.

SEAWEED *is a type of plant that grows and lives in the water. By floating seaweed in water and lifting it out on paper, seaweed will keep its natural shape and design.*

DRIED ARRANGEMENT

MATERIALS:
plant materials such as –
 dried grasses, weeds, seed heads
plaster of Paris
water
small containers, such as –
 paper cups or aluminum pie plates

◆ adult help

ART EXPERIMENT:
1. Collect plant materials in the fall when they are naturally dried in fields and forests.
2. In a paper cup or aluminum pie plate, mix the plaster of Paris with water as described on the bag (or until like whipped cream).
3. When plaster begins to harden, stick the collected dried weeds, grasses, and seed heads into the plaster like a vase full of flowers. Work quickly, as the plaster of Paris will harden rapidly. (Practice arranging materials in a lump of clay before mixing the plaster if desired.)
4. When complete, allow the arrangement to dry overnight.

VARIATIONS:
- While flowers and seed stalks are still green, cut them and hang them upside down with string to dry. When dried, use them in the above project instead of grasses and weeds.
- For a more professional flower arrangement, use a flower pot plastic liner which will fit in a basket, small wooden crate, box, or flower pot.

Plaster of Paris is a white powder made from a crushed rock called GYPSUM.
Adding water to the powdered crushed gypsum makes a thick paste that can be shaped or poured. When it dries, the plaster of Paris becomes a hard, solid material much like the original gypsum rock. Plaster of Paris is a quick-drying art medium for permanent, rock-like uses.

NATURE WINDOWS

MELTING

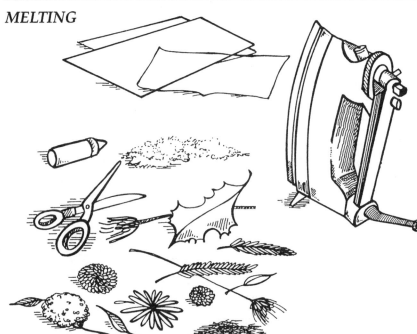

MATERIALS:

newspapers

table

2 sheets plain paper

2 pieces waxed paper

dried or pressed flowers, grasses, leaves

crayon shavings

sand

old iron

scissors

◆ adult help

ART EXPERIMENT:

1. Place a pad of newspaper on the table to protect the table from the heat of the iron.
2. Put one sheet of plain paper on the newspaper.
3. Place one sheet of waxed paper on the plain paper.
4. Arrange dried flowers, grasses, leaves, and crayon shavings in any design on the waxed paper. Finish the design with a tiny sprinkling of sand.
5. Place the second sheet of waxed paper over the design, and the second sheet of plain paper over the waxed paper.
6. An adult will press the design with an old iron on a low setting, pressing firmly and slowly. (The two sheets of waxed paper will melt together.)
7. Remove waxed paper design from between papers and trim edges with scissors.
8. Display the design in a window so the light can shine from the outside in during the day, and from the inside out during the dark night.

VARIATIONS:

- Add bits of ribbon, fabric, lace, glitter, or confetti.
- Make this same design on the sticky side of a sheet of clear contact paper. Then cover the design with another sheet of clear contact paper. Do not iron. Trim the edges.

Waxed paper is just what it sounds like – paper with a coating of wax. The wax on the paper is usually a solid material but MELTS easily into a liquid when heated by the iron which means the wax molecules flow and move around more freely. If the two sheets of waxed paper are touching when heat is applied from the iron and the molecules are moving about, the wax from one sheet will melt and run together with wax from the second sheet. When the heat is removed, the wax papers cool and the molecules arrange themselves in an orderly pattern. The wax becomes solid again, but the two sheets of waxed paper have fused together in one new solid wax.

GARDEN SCULPTURE

MATERIALS:

small clay saucer (the kind under flower pots)
crayons
potting soil
large spoon
grass seed (handful)

spray bottle filled with water
small shells
beeswax
tiny branches

ART EXPERIMENT:

1. Decorate the outside of the clay saucer with crayons.
2. Spoon potting soil into saucer, filling about 3/4 full. (Using hands works well too.)
3. Spray soil with the water to moisten.
4. With hands, sprinkle on a good layer of grass seed, but not too thick.
5. Cover the seed with a thin layer of soil.
6. Spray again with water.
7. Place the saucer in a sunny window and watch for signs of growth.
8. Spray the garden once a day.
9. When the garden has sprouted, add other decorations to the sculpture to imitate a miniature garden. Some suggestions are:
   – tiny branch to look like a tree
   – shells to make a pond (fill with water)
   – small animal made from beeswax

VARIATIONS:

- Stick blossoms of paper on the tiny tree.
- Use a partly buried cosmetic mirror for a pond.
- Add little figurines or toys.
- Add a "log" made from a small stick.
- Make a stone path.
- Grow other small plants as well as grass.

All plants need moisture and sunlight to grow. Grass seeds GERMINATE or sprout and start to grow when water soaks into the seed's covering and food is produced in the seed. After the grass seed germinates, it will continue to need water and light to grow and survive.

FOOD PAINTS

PIGMENT

MATERIALS:

mustard, paprika, cocoa, blackberries, curry, beets, red currants
paper
water
paintbrushes

ART EXPERIMENT:

1. Put spices and foods in individual muffin tin compartments.
2. Add a little water to each compartment and mix well.
3. Dip a paintbrush into the food colors and use this as paint. (People once had to make their own art supplies before art stores were available to buy paint sets. Experiment with making paints from spices, vegetables, and berries. Do not eat these homemade paints.)
4. Rinse brushes often while painting.

VARIATIONS:

- Make paintbrushes from broom-straws, grasses, pine boughs, feathers, or sticks and use these for painting instead of a paintbrush.
- Cook some foods to extract their colors for paint. The following foods work well: beet greens, carrot greens, or cranberries.
- Assemble fruits in a basket and try to paint this still life on paper using food paints.

Foods have natural colorings and dyes called PIGMENTS that have been used throughout history for coloring clothing or for painting. Pigments are CHEMICALS found in food and reflect light the eyes and brain interpret as color. Mixing the foods with water liquifies and thins the foods, making them similar to paints.

HOME PAINTS

CAUTION   **6** *&* *up*

PIGMENTS

MATERIALS:

nuts for brown
daffodils for yellow
beets for red
carrots for orange
grass for green
cranberries for pink

water
stove
sauce pans
paintbrushes
white paper
muffin tin

◆ adult help

ART EXPERIMENT:
1. Boil each of the plants in a separate pan of water until the water turns a deep pretty color. Cool.
2. Pour the colored waters into separate compartments in the muffin tin.
3. Dip a paintbrush in the colored water and paint on white paper.

VARIATIONS:
- Paint with colored water on white fabric.
- Place all the plants in one pot for a strong mixed color.
- Collect other natural materials to use as dyes such as tree bark, flowers, weeds, and grasses.

 The colors seen in the natural world come from chemicals called PIGMENTS. *Pigments are released when the plants are boiled. Since ancient times, plant pigments have been used as dyes for clothes, face paint, and art.*

SAND CLAY

BONDING

> Cornstarch is used in cooking as a thickener. When cornstarch is mixed with sand and water and heated on the stove, the cornstarch works like a cement and thickens the mixture, BONDING the ingredients as a modeling clay which is unlike sand alone or cornstarch alone. When an object made from Sand Clay is dried in the oven or left to dry on a shelf, because the cornstarch has bonded with the sand, the object dries to a rock-hard consistency.

MATERIALS:
one cup of fine beach sand
1/2 cup (125 ml) cornstarch
1/2 cup (125 ml) (and maybe a little more) boiling water
double boiler
stove
flat pan or cookie sheet

◆ adult help

ART EXPERIMENT:
1. An adult can mix the fine beach sand and cornstarch thoroughly in the top of the double boiler on the stove.
2. Next, an adult can pour in the boiling water and mix well.
3. Cook this sand clay mixture in the double boiler briefly until thickened. (If too thick, add a little boiling water.)
4. Cool the sand clay a little bit before modeling. Create any clay designs or objects.
5. Next, place the Sand Clay object on a flat pan in a 275°F (140°C) oven until dry. Or, dry the Sand Clay object for several days on a shelf or table.

VARIATIONS:
• Use Sand Clay to make beach objects such as a shell, crab, boat, castle, or fish.
• This recipe doubles nicely for more Sand Clay.

RESOURCES AND INDEX
chapter 6

RECOMMENDED RESOURCE BOOKS

Ardley, Neil. THE SCIENCE BOOK OF AIR. New York, NY: Harcourt, Brace and Jovanovich, 1991.
ISBN 0-15-200578-1

Ardley, Neil. THE SCIENCE BOOK OF COLOR. New York, NY: Harcourt, Brace and Jovanovich, 1991.
ISBN 0-15-200576-5

Ardley, Neil. THE SCIENCE BOOK OF LIGHT. New York, NY: Harcourt, Brace and Jovanovich, 1991.
ISBN 0-15-200577-3

Ardley, Neil. THE SCIENCE BOOK OF WATER. New York, NY: Harcourt, Brace and Jovanovich, 1991.
ISBN 0-15-200575-7

Barber, Nicola and Keegan, Thomas. 175 MORE SCIENCE EXPERIMENTS. New York, NY: Random House, 1990.
ISBN 0-679-80390-4

Brown, Sam. BUBBLES, RAINBOWS, AND WORMS. Mt. Rainier, MD: Gryphon House, Inc., 1981.
ISBN 0-87659-100-4

Caney, Steven. PLAY BOOK. New York, NY: Workman Publishing, 1975.
ISBN 0-911104-38-0

Caney, Steven. TOY BOOK. New York, NY: Workman Publishing, 1972.
ISBN 0-911104-17-8

Carson, Mary Stetten. THE SCIENTIFIC KID. New York, NY: Perennial Library, 1989.
ISBN 0-06-096316-6

Cobb, Vicki. SCIENCE EXPERIMENTS YOU CAN EAT. New York, NY: Harper Collins, 1972.
ISBN 0-397-31253-9

Cohen, Lynn. AIR AND SPACE. Palo Alto, CA: Monday Morning Books, Inc., 1988.
ISBN 0-912107-80-4

Devito, Alfred and Krockover, Gerald H. CREATIVE SCIENCING. Boston, MA: Little, Brown and Company, 1980.
ISBN 0-316-18161-7

Edom, Helen. SCIENCE WITH WATER. London, England: Usborne House, 1990.
ISBN 0-7460-0604-7

Fiarotta, Phyllis. SNIPS & SNAILS & WALNUT WHALES. New York, NY: Workman Publishing, 1975.
ISBN 0-911104-30-5

Forte, Imogene and Frank, Marjorie. PUDDLES AND WINGS AND GRAPEVINE SWINGS. Nashville, TN: Incentive Publications, 1982.
ISBN 0-86530-004-0

Gaither, Gloria and Dobson, Shirley. LET'S MAKE A MEMORY. Waco, TX: Word Books, 1983.
ISBN 0-8499-2966-0

Granseth, Sandra and McMillen, Diana. BUGS, BUGS, BUGS. Des Moines, IA: Better Homes and Garden Books, 1989.
ISBN 0-696-01884-5

Hann, Judith. HOW SCIENCE WORKS. Pleasantville, NY: Reader's Digest, 1991.
ISBN 0-89577-382-1

Herberholz, Barbara, and Hanson, Lee. EARLY CHILDHOOD ART. Dubuque, IA: William C. Brown Publishers, 1990.
ISBN 0-697-06863-8

Hodgson, Harriet. TOYWORKS. Palo Alto, CA: Monday Morning Books, 1986.
ISBN 0-912107040-5

Howard, Lori A. WHAT TO DO WITH A SQUIRT OF GLUE. Nashville, TN: Incentive Publications, 1987.
ISBN 0-86530-086-0

Javna, John. 50 SIMPLE THINGS YOU CAN DO TO SAVE THE EARTH. Kansas City, MO: Andrews and McMeel, 1990.
ISBN 0-8362-2301-2

Karnes, Merle B. EARLY CHILDHOOD RESOURCE BOOK. Tucson, AZ: Communications Skill Builders, 1985.
ISBN 0-88450-931-1

Keegan, Thomas. 175 AMAZING NATURE EXPERIMENTS. New York, NY: Random House, 1991.
ISBN 0-679-82043-4

Kerrod, Robin. AIR IN ACTION. New York, NY: Marshall Cavendish, 1990.
ISBN 1-85435-152-4

Kerrod, Robin. FIRE AND WATER. New York, NY: Marshall Cavendish, 1990.
ISBN 1-85435-153-2

Kerrod, Robin. HOW THINGS WORK. New York, NY: Marshall Cavendish, 1990.
ISBN 1-85435-154-0

Kerrod, Robin. IS IT MAGIC? New York, NY: Marshall Cavendish, 1990.
ISBN 1-85435-155-9

Kerrod, Robin. LIGHT FANTASTIC. New York,NY: Marshall Cavendish, 1990.
ISBN 1-85435-156-7

Kohl, MaryAnn F. and Gainer, Cindy. GOOD EARTH ART. Bellingham, WA:
Bright Ring Publishing, 1991.
ISBN 0-935607-01-3

Kohl, MaryAnn F. MUDWORKS. Bellingham, WA: Bright Ring Publishing, 1988.
ISBN 0-935607-02-1

Kohl, MaryAnn F. SCRIBBLE COOKIES. Bellingham, WA: Bright Ring Publishing,
1985.
ISBN 0-935607-10-2

Knox, Gerald M. WATER WONDERS. Des Moines, IA: Better Homes and Garden
Books, 1989.
ISBN 0-696-01883-7

Lanners, Edi. SECRETS OF 123 CLASSIC SCIENCE TRICKS AND EXPERIMENTS.
Blue Ridge Summit, PA: TAB Books, 1987.
ISBN 0-8306-2821-5

Miller, Karen. THE OUTSIDE PLAY AND LEARNING BOOK. Mt. Rainier, MD:
Gryphon House, Inc., 1989.
ISBN 0-87659-117-9

Milord, Susan. THE KIDS' NATURE BOOK. Charlotte, VT: Williamson Publishing,
1989.
ISBN 0-9133589-42-X

Nichols, Wendy and Nichols, Kim. WONDERSCIENCE. Santa Fe, NM: Learning
Expo Publishing, 1990.
ISBN 0-9625907-0-3

Ontario Science Centre. SCIENCEWORKS. Reading, MA: Addison-Wesley
Publishing Company, Inc., 1986.
ISBN 0-2-1-16780-8

Paula, Nancy. HELPING YOUR CHILD LEARN SCIENCE. Washington, DC: US
Department of Education, Office of Educational Research and Improvement,
1992.

Penrose, Gordon. SENSATIONAL SCIENCE ACTIVITIES. New York, NY: Simon &
Schuster, Inc., 1990.
ISBN 0-671-72552-1

Petrash, Carol. EARTHWAYS. Mt. Rainier, MD: Gryphon House, Inc., 1992.
ISBN 0-87659-156-X

Potter, Jean. JEAN POTTER'S RECIPES FOR EARLY LEARNING. Palm Springs,
CA: In-Print Publications, 1992.

Rockwell, Robert. HUG A TREE. Mt. Rainier, MD: Gryphon House, Inc., 1986.
ISBN 0-87659-105-5

Schwartz, Linda. EARTH BOOK FOR KIDS. Santa Barbara, CA: The Learning
Works, 1990.
ISBN 0-88160-195-0

Sherwood, Elizabeth; Williams, Robert; and Rockwell, Robert. MORE MUDPIES TO
MAGNETS. Mt. Rainier, MD: Gryphon House, Inc., 1990.
ISBN 0-87659-150-0

Sisson, Edith A. NATURE WITH CHILDREN OF ALL AGES. New York, NY:
Prentice Hall Press, 1982.
ISBN 0-13-611542

Smithsonian Institution. MORE SCIENCE ACTIVITIES. Annapolis, MD: Science
Learning, Inc., 1988.
ISBN 0-939456-16-8

Stacy, Dennis. NIFTY AND THRIFTY SCIENCE ACTIVITIES. Carthage, IL: Fearon
Teacher Aids, 1988.
ISBN 0-8224-4777-0

Stangl, Jean. SCIENCE LESSONS AND EXPERIMENTS USING WATER. Carthage,
IL: Fearon Teaching Aids, 1990.
ISBN 0-8224-3604-3

Stein, Sara. THE SCIENCE BOOK. New York, NY: Workman Publishing, 1980.
ISBN 0-089480-120

Van Cleave, Janice. 200 GOOEY, SLIPPERY, SLIMY, WEIRD & FUN
EXPERIMENTS. New York, NY: John Wiley & Sons, Inc., 1992.
ISBN 0-471-57921-1

Walpole, Brenda. 175 SCIENCE EXPERIMENTS. New York, NY: Random House,
1988.
ISBN 0-394-89991-1

Wilkes, Angela. MY FIRST NATURE BOOK. New York, NY: Alfred A. Knopf, 1990.
ISBN 0-394-86610-X

Wilkes, Angela. MY FIRST SCIENCE BOOK. New York, NY: Afred A. Knopf, 1990.
ISBN 0-679-80583-4

Wilkes, Angela and Mostyn, David. SIMPLE SCIENCE. Tulsa, OK: EDC Publishing,
1983.
ISBN 0-86020-761-7

Willow, Diane and Curran, Emily. SCIENCE SENSATIONS. Reading, MA:
Addison-Wesley Publishing Company, Inc., 1989.
ISBN 0-201-07189-4

CONCEPT INDEX

acid: A material that tastes sour, reacts with bases, and turns purple cabbage juice red. *Invisible Paint 110; Magic Cabbage 111*

adhesion/cohesion: Molecules are attracted to the molecules of other materials by a force called adhesion. Molecules are held together by a stronger force called cohesion. *Candle Coloring 94; White Resist 95*

air: A colorless, odorless, tasteless, gaseous mixture of elements that supports life on Earth. Contains nitrogen, oxygen, other gases, pollutants, and a variety of tiny particles of materials. *Sticky Pictures 119*

attract: Pull towards, as with magnets. *See magnetism.*

base: A material that tastes bitter, reacts with acids, and turns purple cabbage juice green. *Invisible Paint 110; Magic Cabbage 111*

buoyancy: The upward force that a liquid exerts on an object. The force is equal to the weight of the liquid that is pushed aside when the object enters the liquid. *Floating Sculpture 34*

casein: A white plastic-like substance made from milk. *Plastic Milk 105*

centrifugal force: The force on a spinning object from the center (or axis) out and away from the center. *Twirling Rainbow 73*

chlorophyll: Green pigments found in plants that trap energy from sunlight. *Grass Patterns 123*

chromatography: Separating mixtures through an absorbent material at different rates. *Chromatography 97*

condensation: Tiny drops of water on cold things which form when water vapor in the air cools and turns back into water. *See evaporation.*

constellation: A pattern made by stars in the sky. One common constellation is the Big Dipper. *Star Window 66*

crystals: Ice, salt, and many kinds of minerals are all crystals with definite internal structures and external shapes arranged in patterns. *Frost Plate 20; Crystal Sparkle Dough 37; Crystal Design 100; Crystal Paint 101; Crystal Bubbles 102; Crystal Needles 103; Crystal Ink 104*

density: The measurement of the weight of a specific volume; a scientific way to compare the compact character of a material. *Oil & Water Painting 18; Oil Painting 19; Bottle Optics 30; Water Tube 31; Floating Sculpture 34; Clay Floats 35*

diffusion: Spontaneous movement of molecules from one place to another with a uniform mixture resulting. Food coloring diffuses in water. *Wet Paint Design 14; Wet and Dry Painting 15; Rain Dancer 24; Color Bottles 28*

dissolve: The complete mixing of a solid in a liquid which then forms a new substance. When sugar dissolves in water, the new substance is sugar water. *Wet and Dry Painting 15; Oil Painting 19; Spaghetti Painting 108*

electricity: A form of energy. *Motor Car Print 84*

emulsion: A suspension of small globules of one liquid in a second liquid with which the first will not mix, such as milk fats in milk. *Color Waves 36; Erupting Colors 98*

energy: Power, as shown in action, exertion, performance, or movement. *Shake Picture 70; Gear Sculpture 77*

engineering: Design, construction, and operation of structures, equipment, and systems. *Marshmallow Tower 106; Building Beans 107*

evaporate: The change from a liquid to a gas by increasing the heat content of the liquid. *Water Painting 17; Paper Molds 33; Crystal Ink 104*

filter: To separate solids or suspended particles from a liquid by passing it through a layer of sand, fiber, or charcoal. Light can also be filtered through colored paper or thin fabric. *Color Viewing Box 64*

freezing point: The temperature at which a liquid solidifies. Water freezes at 32°F (0°C). *Frost Plate 20; Frozen Paper 21; Cube Painting 22; Colored Ice Cubes 23; Ice Structures 26; Crystal Paint 101; Crystal Bubbles 102*

friction: The resistance met by the rubbing together of one material on the surface of another material. *Paint Racing 71; Polished Crayon 80*

gases: Matter which has low density, expands and contracts readily, and distributes uniformly through any container. *The Volcano 99; Sculptured Pretzels 112*

gears: Combinations of wheels with teeth around the edge that work on each other to effect movement. *Gear Sculpture 77*

germinate: To sprout or start to sprout and grow from a seed. Water and sunlight are necessary for germination. *Garden Sculpture 129*

gluten: A glue-like substance found in flour. *Spaghetti Painting 108*

gnomon: The part of a sundial which casts a shadow and helps measure time. *Shadow Time 53*

gravity: The strength of attraction between two objects because of their mass and distance. The earth's gravity pulls everything toward its center. *Paint Racing 71; Marble Sculpture 76; Paint Pendulum 78; Salt Pendulum 79; Moon Scape 85*

image: The light seen when it bounces off a surface. In a mirror, the reflection bounces off as an image. *See reflection.*

immiscible: Two liquids cannot mix. Oil is immiscible in water. *Immiscibles 96*

inertia: The tendency of something to stay still or keep moving. Gravity and friction can affect inertia. *Marble Sculpture 76*

insoluble: Cannot be dissolved or mixed. Oil and water will not mix even when shaken or stirred. *Invisible Designs 16; Oil & Water Painting 18; Oil Painting 19; Color Waves 36*

light: A form of energy; part of the electromagnetic spectrum. *Tissue Color Mix 50; White Color Wheel 51*

liquid: A state of matter where molecules move freely.

magnet: An object which can attract or repel certain materials. *Magnet Painting 88; Funny Faces 89; Metallic Design 90; Magnetic Stage Play 91; Magnetic Rubbing 92*

magnetic field: The area around a magnet in which the force of the magnet affects the movement of other magnetic objects. *Magnet Painting 88; Funny Faces 89; Metallic Design 90; Magnetic Stage Play 91; Magnetic Rubbing 92*

magnetic force field: The area around a magnet that attracts magnetic materials. *Magnet Painting 88; Funny Faces 89; Metallic Design 90; Magnetic Stage Play 91; Magnetic Rubbing 92*

magnetism: Invisible force that attracts or repels magnetic materials and has electromagnetic effects. *Magnet Painting 88; Funny Faces 89; Metallic Design 90; Magnetic Stage Play 91; Magnetic Rubbing 92*

melting point: The point at which a solid material will begin to turn to a liquid. The melting point of ice is 32°F (0°C). *Cube Painting 22; Colored Ice Cubes 23; Ice Structures 26; Ice & Salt Sculpture 27; Polished Crayon 80; Crayon Creatures 81; Hot Sand Paper 82; Baked Drawings 83; Nature Windows 128*

molecule: The tiny particle produced by the linking of two or more atoms. Everything is made up of tiny particles called molecules.

opaque: Not allowing rays of light to pass through; cannot be seen through. *Overhead Outlines 56; Silhouettes 60; Silhouette Show 61; Flashlight Patterns 62; Window Scene 67*

optical illusion: The brain "sees" an image in a way that tricks the eye into seeing the object a different way. One common optical illusion is when lines are drawn very close together and they appear to the brain to be moving when they are really holding still. *Spinning Designs 45; Hidden Coloring 45; Secret Pictures 46; Stretch Picture 47; Dot Matrix Picture 48; Face Illusion 49; Streak Spin 72; Moving Pets 74; Spoke Weaving 75*

pendulum: A weighted rod or string fixed at one end which swings freely. *Paint Pendulum 78; Salt Pendulum 79*

photography: The process of creating optical images on photosensitive surfaces, such as on film. *Real Camera 65*

pigments: Any substance or matter used as coloring. Often found naturally in foods and plants used as dyes, inks, and paints. *Tissue color Mix 50; Plant Imprints 117; Food Paints 130; Home Paints 131*

plants: Any organism, not animal, with cellulose cell walls, that grows, lacks locomotion, and lacks organs or nervous tissue. Usually has roots, blossoms, and leaves and is often green. *Bark Rubbing 114; Shoe Polish Leaves 115; Nature Spray 116; Plant Imprints 117; Stencil Leaves 120; Tree Arts 121; Grass Patterns 123; Dried Seaweed Print 126; Dried Arrangement 127; Garden Sculpture 129; Food Paints 130; Home Paints 131*

pointillism: An art technique of applying paint in small dots or points to the paper in order to create an effect of optical mixing. The painter, Seurat, is famous for pointillism. *Dot Matrix Picture 48*

pressure: Force applied over a surface or the application of continuous force. *Bottle Fountain 29; Crystal Sparkle Dough 37; Straw Painting 38; The Volcano 99*

reflection: The light or image seen when light bounces off a surface. *See It Cards 52; Infinity Reflection 54; Mirror Painting 55; Color and Shine 57; Flashlight Reflections 63; Bubble Sculpture 68*

repel: To push away, as with magnets. *See magnetism.*

rocks: Any relatively hard, naturally formed mass of minerals or petrified material. Sand is mostly crushed or ground up rock. *Sand Drawings 124; Sand Garden 125; Dried Arrangement 127; Sand Clay 132*

solid: A substance that is compact; not liquid.

soluble: Can be dissolved, such as salt in water. *Wet and Dry Painting 15; Erupting Colors 98*

solution: Liquid containing a dissolved substance. *See dissolve.*

spectrum: The colors found in white light – red, orange, yellow, green, blue, indigo, and violet. *White Color Wheel 51*

static electricity: A buildup of negative charges called electrons. Static means it stays in one place, unlike current electricity, which can flow through things. *Balloon Decoration 86; Dancing Rabbits 87*

sundial: A tool for telling the time on a sunny day by the shadows cast each hour. *Shadow Time 53*

surface tension: The stretchy skin of a liquid which is caused by the attraction of molecules on its surface. *Chalk Float Design 25; Color Waves 36*

symmetry: Balance, matching arrangement of pattern, or equal and exact matching. *Flowing Patterns 32; Symmetry Prints 118*

texture: The appearance and feel of something. Sandpaper has a rough texture. A mirror has a smooth texture. *Sandpaper Designs 109*

time: A way to measure an hour, day, month, or year based on the rotation and revolution of the Earth. *Shadow Time 53*

translucent: Light can shine through but cannot be seen through. *Color and Shine 57; Slide Viewer 58; Slide Show 59; Window Scene 67; Nature Windows 128*

transparent: Light can shine through and can be seen through. *Color and Shine 57; Flashlight Patterns 62; Nature Windows 128*

water vapor: Tiny droplets of water in the air too small to see and formed by evaporation. *See evaporation.*

weathering: The grinding action that makes sand. *Sand Drawings 124*

white light: A band of seven different colors – red, orange, yellow, green, blue, indigo, and violet. Each color has a different wavelength. All the colors mixed together make white light. *White Color Wheel 51*

wind: Movement of air. *Streamer Rings 39; Wind Catcher 40; Windy Wrap 41; Wind Chime 42*

INDEX

MATERIALS INDEX

The Materials Index can be helpful in several ways:

1. Use as a checklist to see which projects match up with materials and supplies you already have or can easily find.

2. Use as a guide for materials to compile for future art experiences.

3. When you remember a material you've used in a project, but not the name of the project, use the Index to find that project and its page number.

NOTE: Basic supplies such as scissors, glues, paper, and paint are not listed unless used as a unique or unusual part of the art experience.

ABOUT THE AUTHORS

MaryAnn Kohl received a BS in Elementary Education from Old Dominion University, Virginia, with graduate studies from Western Washington State University. Her interest in creative art for children comes from years of teaching elementary and preschool children, using a whole language and learning center approach. MaryAnn is the author of the award winning books in art for children: *Scribble Cookies, Mudworks,* and *Good Earth Art.* In addition to writing, she works as an educational consultant in art, illustrating, and publishing for young authors. MaryAnn is the owner of Bright Ring Publishing. She lives with her husband and two daughters in Bellingham, Washington where she enjoys the outdoors, reading, and family activities.

Jean Potter graduated from Edinboro University in Pennsylvania with a BS in Early Childhood Education and a Master of Arts and Sciences in Early Childhood and Television Communications from West Virginia University. Her professional responsibilities included teaching kindergarten, coordinating and directing the early childhood education program for the West Virginia State Department of Education, and teaching at a variety of colleges and universities. Most recently Jean was the Deputy Assistant Secretary, then Acting Assistant Secretary, of Elementary and Secondary Education for the U.S. Department of Education. She is currently involved in writing and developing educational materials for parents and teachers. She lives in Charleston, West Virginia with her husband, Thomas, and enjoys walking her Welsh Corgie, Archie.

BRIGHT IDEAS BOOKSHELF

11 X 8-1/2 • 144 pages • $15.95 • paper
ISBN 0-935607-04-8

11 X 8-1/2 • 224 pages • $16.95 • paper
ISBN 0-935607-01-3

11 X 8-1/2 • 152 pages • $14.95 • paper
ISBN 0-935607-02-1

11 X 8-1/2 • 144 pages • $12.95 • paper
ISBN 0-935607-10-2

Children 3-10 learn basic science concepts as they explore over 100 amazing and beautiful art experiences using common household materials. Projects are open-ended and easy to do. One science-art experiment per page, fully illustrated. Includes three indexes and a charted Table of Contents. Suitable for home, school, or child care.

Over 200 art projects that develop an awareness of the environment and a caring attitude towards the earth. Uses common materials collected from nature or recycled from trash. Filled with simple ideas to recycle and create for all ages. Includes charted Table of Contents, two indexes, and a list of environmental resources.
1992 Benjamin Franklin Award

Anyone who likes to play in mud, playdough, papier-mache and similar mediums will love this book of over 125 clays, doughs, and modeling mixtures. Uses common household materials and requires no expertise. Ideal for fun or serious art for all ages, for home or school.
1991 Benjamin Franklin Award
1990 American Library Assn. Starred Review

Over 100 process art ideas that stress exploration in an independent, non-competitive, open-ended setting. Activities need only basic art supplies and common kitchen materials. Ideal for any age, for home or school.

1991 Daycare Directors Choice Award